THE
SACRED
PURPOSE
OF
BEING HUMAN

A Journey Through the 12 Principles of Wholeness

Jacquelyn Small

Health Communications, Inc.
Deerfield Beach, Florida

www.bcibooks.com

Library of Congress Cataloging-in-Publication Data

Small, Jacquelyn.
    The sacred purpose of being human : a journey through the
12 principles of wholeness / Jacquelyn Small.
        p. cm.
    Includes bibliographical references.
    ISBN 0-7573-0330-7
    1. Spiritual life. 2. Holism. 3. Whole and parts (Psychology)
    4. Whole and parts (Philosophy) I. Title.

BL624.S59465 2005
204'.4—dc22

                                            2005046098

Publisher: Health Communications, Inc.
            3201 S.W. 15th Street
            Deerfield Beach, FL 33442-8190

Cover design by Andrea Perrine Brower
Inside book design by Lawna Patterson Oldfield
Inside book formatting by Dawn Von Strolley Grove

CONTENTS

IN
APPRECIATION

To Carl Gustav Jung, Roberto Assagioli, Sri Aurobindo, and the Tibetan Master Djwhal Khul, my greatest teachers and inspiration, ... who, without their remarkable understanding of the human psyche, I could never have written a book.

To Peter Vegso and Gary Seidler of Health Communications ... for believing in me.

To my editor and "copilot," Penelope Love ... who brought her enthusiasm, integrity and crystal clarity to the writing of this book.

To Brenda Shea, my "right arm" in the grounding and implementation of the Eupsychia Process, our national psychospiritual healing and training program ... whose dedication and deep understanding of me and this work has made it possible.

To my staff and students of Eupsychia Institute ... whose willingness to do inner work, and help guide it, have provided me the living laboratory for a loving, hands-on study of the Self.

To my family, all of you, ... for your understanding and support of my life's work. And especially to my three-year-old granddaughter, Margaret Jacquelyn, who teaches me daily, with such innocence, the thrill of being human.

PREFACE

In my spiritual training years ago, I came across some words of the English metaphysical historian, Gareth Knight, that caused everything to fall into place about who we are and why we are here. He said that it is the refusal to come down to Earth, literally, that is the cause of the bulk of spiritual pathology and the root of all disease, ignorance, and what we call "sin." It is a rejection of the work of our Father in heaven, he claimed, explaining that until physical existence is seen and willingly entered into as sacred, we will never fulfill our purpose here. So even though we know it is spiritual factors that operate behind everything created, we must never use this knowledge to remove ourselves from being fully in this world or to see human life as beneath us or improper in any way. To do this violates our sacred purpose for being here.[1]

God obviously created the human kingdom. So human, we are supposed to be. While on Earth, we are here to come fully into ourselves as spiritual beings living in human bodies, with the awareness that our purpose is to bring spirit into all our human ways. God *spiritualizes matter;* we, as God's ambassadors to Earth, are here to *materialize spirit.* This is our sacred purpose for having taken on the human condition. And though this planet is in a tragic state of chaos and deep sorrow, we are to stick with it, no matter what.

Perhaps as we've traveled through the human condition we've gotten stuck in the human process and can't remember how to move on. We so easily get drawn into unconscious behavior that takes us down instead of up. I certainly know I do at times. Yet, deep in our hearts, we all know there is something of mysterious value about the very act of being human. Even though we see so much suffering here, surely we're not to be considered God's mistake! So what is the cause of so much hatred, pain, and warring chaos here? Why is it we have so much trouble just loving each other and creating a peaceful world?

HUMANITY'S EMOTIONAL BODY NEEDS HEALING

Nearly every day I hear from people who are deeply troubled from some aspect of living in this complex and often callous world—seeking recovery from disillusionment, betrayal, sorrow, addictions, or loss of meaning and spirit. And I've seen so plainly that when people are suffering from guilt, shame or loss of hope from having made some serious mistake, the underlying feeling is that it's simply wrong to be human. There's so often a serious split within them between feeling good or evil, saved or unsaved, with the mistaken notion that to be spiritual, we should just leave these unclean human bodies, rise above it all, and burst into light. In all this confusion, it's easy to lose one's passion or purpose for living. It seems to me that as humanity has traveled its journey through time, we've collected more and more emotional "debris" that has never been accessed, made conscious, and healed. The tendency, then, is to project all these emotional wounds and imbalances onto others, or else become hopeless, filled with shame, guilt and piles of self-doubt.

Negative emotions build upon themselves, creating more and more misery and misunderstanding. Anytime our life starts running off course, we tend to move from one extreme to another in our feeling nature. Every human affliction can be seen as some form of either "too little" or "too much" of something that imbalances one's emotional life. We vacillate from emotional flatness to excessive cravings; from sexual or relational avoidance to sexual and romantic obsessions; from mental rigidity to over-stimulation; and on up into the heights of spiritual emptiness or fanaticism. Through these imbalanced emotions, we then actually create "story lines" based on how we feel. As a therapist, I've observed that people can even become addicted to their own suffering and will unconsciously set about creating more and more of it.

Yet, here's some very good news. Science is starting to validate the importance of our need for emotional happiness, even to our physical health. Research in the area of mind/body medicine is now replete with how we store repressed emotions in our neuro-chemical network, which then become addictive. They're finding also that the brain cannot tell the difference between a memory and an actual here-and-now event in terms of how it processes the information. Therefore, memories held in our body/mind become the stimuli for addictive emotional reactions to spontaneously burst forth. Our emotions, we now know, are the driving force that guide our behavior and the choices that we make.[2]

These reactions that come from unprocessed emotions are signs we are still partially living in the past. Our present emotional life will then be contaminated everywhere there is an overlap between a present experience and a memory from our earlier life. Unconscious, distorted emotions must be brought to consciousness for a stable healing to occur and for us to awaken in truth. Often I hear people say they are desperately seeking ways to step out of their past and be no longer burdened by old issues that remain unhealed.

When we can clear our emotional bodies, we become "transparent," able to live completely in the now with integrity and more joy of being alive. We not only leave behind our little personal stories that keep us stuck in the past, but we help to re-shape humanity by modeling a more inspired and integrated life. All of humanity is swimming in a sea of unclean emotional waters. And the healing of our species must begin with each of us.

For our human psyche's well-being, it's urgent that we learn to live more into our bigger story, into the life of our soul. This higher, more refined way of living ushers in a much more potent, down-to-earth spiritual life where a daily practice of just being ourselves empowers and strengthens this newfound higher identity. To gain true knowledge of something we must enter into complete union with it; we must actually experience that which is to be known.

For years, in our healing programs with hundreds who come from all walks of life, we've observed how transformations occur naturally through emotional release and grounding our thoughts in the real truth of our nature. I'm convinced that a call has gone out, perhaps from our very soul, and some kind of new life is straining to come forth. Writing this book is my way of sharing with you what I'm learning from all the spiritual seekers I'm so fortunate to meet and work with—about who we are and why we are here.

A MISSING LINK

Though many people do reach out for help today with personal issues or floundering relationships, it is obvious to me that something basic has been missing, not only in our personal and work lives, but in a lot of health care and religious institutions as well. From my 30 years of self-exploration and helping others to heal, here's what I've come to believe: We're forgetting how to live the simple, natural way of just being ourselves. Even our psychologies and religious trainings are failing to teach us who we really are and why we've come to Earth. *What's being left out of most human living today is the essential Self, our incarnated soul.* Though we *are* spiritual souls living in human bodies, there's little recognition of this identity as fact.

This means that the very core of our nature capable of inspiring, healing and transforming us is being virtually ignored. We are fixated on the ego here, trying to fix it or feed it to make our outer lives more successful. But the ego has never come close to being wise enough to run a human life. Egos don't know how to open our hearts, or take us into a creative, intuitive, spirit-filled life. It is my conviction that this missing link must be addressed if we are to ever experience the bliss of being whole. I believe we are in dire need of an enormous perceptual adjustment, to come back to the essential truth of our nature. We are forgetting who we are.

The process offered as you explore this book can become a pathway for you to access, identify and modify the basic patterns buried in the depths of your psyche that are holding any dysfunction in place. Until we root out our core woundings, these imbalances in our feeling nature continue to re-create themselves in all our relationships and situations.

When our egos start running to the edge of their demise, inside us, our deeper Self, the soul, rises up to overtake the ego's limited ways. When you hit a time of uprooting change in your life, called a transformational cycle, your thoughts will turn toward a yearning to know who you truly are. You'll start to balk at going off into nonessential, time-wasting pursuits, and you'll hear yourself saying things like, "This is not me. What am I doing?" Well, who in you knows that? There is obviously someone inside you who is nudging you to notice that you are bored with your old ways and ready to move on. This is your true Self. This is the wake-up call to step out of any unconscious living as an inauthentic person. This may be what you are feeling right now, and why you picked up this book.

SEEING YOUR HUMAN LIFE AS SACRED

To maintain a healthy motivation to "come clean" from any unhealthy way of living, your life must be imbued with a sense of greater identity and sacred purpose. When you step into your greater Self (that you already are, by the way), your identity actually shifts to a healthier and higher sense of selfhood. You are now observing that one you used to be who had so much trouble. Whether living in a mansion or under a bridge, this identity shift is the key for all recovering human beings—to turn inward and allow the true and greater Self to shine forth, and then to live as that translucent one. This compassionate, essential Self of ours, *when acknowledged as legitimate,* has the power to re-awaken passion and bring spirit back into our lives.

We crave the thrill of impassioned living. When we can no longer feel inspired and creative, our minds go dull and we begin to lose heart. Since we are already filled with so much unused or misdirected passion, why not start today throwing ourselves wholeheartedly into a whole new, life-enhancing way of being, wherever we spend our time? On a path of Self-discovery, there's no one outside us who can do this for us—we must *be* the change we seek.

Just as Jesus modeled for us—as have all the other great beings who've resided here—we must all go through our own crucifixion before a true resurrection and ascension in consciousness can come about. And we each have a soul or internal Guardian to guide us. So we must turn inward to align with the truth of our being. When we turn inward, the great mystery of life is there to greet us.

We are already standing in the Self we came here to be; there are unfortunately, many layers of defenses built around us, blocking us from being it. Yet, no matter how hard we may try to deny it, our very essence is spiritually imbued with life-giving qualities. Our basic nature is not emotional moodiness and reactions; our basic nature is love.

Many of you are ready to know yourselves in a whole new way now and to remember why you came to earth. The kind of processes you'll encounter in these pages are guided by a comprehensive goal: to align with an effective approach to living that offers practical, life-enhancing help for those of you who are seeking not just a set of new skills at living, but a transformed life.

I hope that taking in what's written here will bring you an inspired realization that you are a valuable individual with a unique gift to bring the world. The principles and emotional-healing methods of inner work offered will help to release you from your affliction—no matter what it is—or any kind of persistent self-doubt. You will learn how to create the inner space for spiritual awakenings to occur naturally—without the need of an earth-shaking tragedy to startle you awake. I sincerely hope that this book provides sustenance and loving support for your emotional healing and a renewed sense of purpose. There is indeed a sacred purpose to being human. And it's time we all start remembering this and living as the Self we came here to be.

Perhaps one day we will meet face to face. Until then, may your journey of awakening be filled with thrilling insights and the joy of knowing what a magnificent being you are!

A NOTE TO MY READERS

Our Yearning for Both Spiritual and Earthly Pleasures

We don't so much crave the meaning of life
as we do the rapture of being alive.

—Joseph Campbell

Seeking after "the delights of the flesh" has its most ancient of roots within the human design. And so does having feelings of guilt and wrongness for wanting such pleasures. We tend to separate our human self from our spiritual self, as though one is bad, and the other good. Our inability to understand how to resolve these troublesome opposites within us have led many an unsteady soul into the lure of addiction, neurosis and all kinds of relationship dysfunction—a treacherous road that nobody would ever *consciously* choose to tread. It's natural to love both the sensuous human pleasures and the feelings of being spiritual, or "high." Yet these lusty and lofty pursuits often get us in a great deal of trouble. It's why so many of our youth chase after high consciousness drug experiences, not understanding what they are seeking, and why becoming obsessed with sex, glamour and romance is so prevalent in our illusory human lives. It's why we are a nation of alcohol consumers, or at least where social drinking is the *most* comfortable social norm.

Your passionate nature longs for the numinous, aesthetic experiences of the nonrational subjective life of your soul. We all crave this mysterious and intense involvement with life, and thrill at the sight of beauty, grace and artistic expression. This is the high side of being "an addict." It isn't befitting divine creatures like us to be content with the comfortable norm! When aesthetic living takes hold in your life, your mind will court your heart by deciding to open to the ways of your soul.

This passion for living, every person with a propensity for addiction knows quite well; it's what they've been seeking through chemical and relational highs. The great mythologist Joseph Campbell commented once that "we don't so much crave the meaning of life as we do the rapture of being alive." This rapture comes to us naturally once we find the keys that unlock that precious gift of being turned on already living within us. Our ultimate joy and fulfillment as spiritual beings living in human bodies will never come from outside us. Though we enjoy celebrating our sensual human experiences with each other, at some point, to complete ourselves, we must all turn inward and discover the natural way to attain the peace and joy we've all come here to share.

Human Desire Is a Gift from God

This sacred pathway our cravings and attachments carve through our lives is the subject of this book. We will thoroughly explore the human shadow, our "dark side"—the side of us that brings us shame and much unhappiness—who lives in our emotional body and tries to satisfy our cravings in unconscious, harmful ways. Since the Law of Love is the governing principle while we're on this earth, we can learn to heal the unloved parts of us, and to help each other in our struggles, so we can feel more healthy and whole. From now on, you will notice that any difficulty you ever get into in your life will turn out to be a lesson in Love.

Sadly, many people have not realized that human desire is a God-given quality. The feeling of attraction is the activated Law of Love in all of creation. We love what we desire, and we desire what we love. So, it's this very power of desire that imprints the nature of God, which is Love, upon our lives. There is a driving force in human nature that forever moves us toward sanctifying our desires: we not only yearn for sensual pleasure, we hunger to merge with the divine. It is through this constant feeling of "divine discontent" that we eventually drive ourselves into a replica of our own ideal, our whole Self.

There will always be a kind of "erotic gratification" that accompanies any affair of the heart. To live in divine Love and have Love live in us is so fulfilling, it becomes our highest intention. For in this way, God's nature as Love comes toward us. And we, as made in God's image, become this love in human form—we "take it on." Whenever you are moving forward on this "high road," your life will seem worth living, even when you hit the rough spots. You will feel you are living in God and God is living in you. And this is a state of pure ecstasy.

Natural Transcenders Are Muses of the Soul

You passionate ones are natural transcenders; you are the muses of the soul. You can learn to love and accept yourselves as the lucky possessors of hearty appetites, hungry minds and hearts that yearn for truth and rapturous living. The craving, the hunt, the heady anticipation of the seeker, of always going toward some deep, intense experience, always seeking a greater joy that brings a deeper wisdom—perhaps this is the true blessing of being alive. And even more: perhaps it's God's way of keeping us on a path of transcendence. For, though we often burn our wings and crash to earth in puddles of heartfelt sorrow or delight, we love to fly high! We are the people of the heart.

It could be that this is why our future continually beckons but never really arrives. Our "divine discontent" assures us that we'll never rest in any sort of incomplete state—and keeps us feeling that we're always capable of going beyond our current possibilities, again, and again, and again. Perhaps this is how we eventually simulate our God-nature and become our own ideal.

Acceptance of your whole nature as both human and divine requires a shift in consciousness that cannot be taken for granted; a great deal of inner work must be employed before you can actually resolve these "devilish" splits inside you that can literally tear you apart. Have you ever thought about how much simple self-acceptance is the key to your well-being? Once your emotional body heals, your self-acceptance is assured.

I've written this book to offer you much validation and support for your healing process and acceptance of yourself just as you are—and right where you are—on your journey home.

Warmest regards,
Jacquelyn Small
January 2005

INTRODUCTION

Today something is happening
to the whole structure of human consciousness.
A rich kind of life is starting.

—Pierre Tielhard de Chardin

It's true! I see rapid, positive changes happening in folks all around me. What if a year from now (or sooner), *you* could look back and see that you've become the person you'd always wanted to be? You notice you're no longer so ruled by your past, that your relationships are no longer tainted by unhealed issues. You feel a reawakened passion for living your life, inspired and creative again. This has happened to many I know, and it can happen for you.

Reading books on transformational inner work differs from ordinary reading. They are living truth, not "dead letter." The messages encapsulated in this book (especially in the 12 Principles of Wholeness) are layered, such that different aspects of meaning will stir you at differing times, depending on what level of consciousness you're on as you encounter them. You will hear what you need to hear when you need to hear it, and discover new per-spectives as you deepen your awareness of Self.

The chapters on the 12 Principles of Wholeness you'll study in this book can be a 12-month process of personal transformation. You might decide to use this book as a 12-month daily guide and meditation, working with each Principle for a whole month. Each Principle functions as a "seed thought" that will gradually take root in your mind as you walk consciously through each day practicing living from each of them. They will keep you grounded in your whole and true Self. Or, you can simply read the book and gain from it what you will. Either way, this book evokes a transforma-tional process. The teachings and experiences you'll meet here are designed to bring you the richness of a regular life filled with all kinds of thrilling adventures in consciousness—if you are willing to enter into them with *radical* self-honesty and purposeful inten-tion.

The transformational inner work in this book has been tried and proved by many of your brother and sister souls who have studied with us through the years. The psychospiritual processes included here will help you balance a lot of your karma (the consequences of your actions that have collected over the years from uncon-scious living), so that you can take your next step in your life's true expression. If you feel drawn to what's being said here but have felt isolated in your thinking, here's some information that might help you feel less alone:

Research indicates that there are some 50 million people in the United States today forming a new subculture interested in expe-riential personal growth and transformation, and in creative prob-lem solving for the making of a better world.[3] These are not "new agers" or dropouts from society. They are scientists, architects, uni-versity professors, novelists, artists, homemakers, physicians and other opinion-makers. As Richard Florida describes in *The Creative Class,* they like to engage in work whose function is to "create meaningful new forms." And these researchers speculate that these "cultural creatives" may be reshaping our larger culture as well. You are the folks, I believe, who are stepping out of old, fragmented ways of being and coming into your true selves.

We've gone as far as we can in our separatist ways of living ego-centered lives. As you can see, we're unconsciously destroying our planet as well as our quality of life. The Self, our true nature, is calling us now to wake up and take responsibility for becoming healthy and whole human beings. We are evolving into our next and greater identity. *The Sacred Purpose of Being Human* is about creating your meaningful new form and aligning with your innate spiritual power to pursue your life's dream. It's about taking a journey inward to discover the creative, spirit-filled Self.

As your soul awakens, you begin to view yourself broadly "from on high." You'll start living your greater story, seeing the sacred purpose behind everything that's happened to you, even your worst "mistakes." This philosophy of wholeness will enable you to recognize and express the potential that already resides within you— it is just awaiting your notice. There is magic in the methods you'll encounter here. I know, because I've done them for years while also witnessing the results of many others. Now I'm inviting you to join this radical recovery and revitalizing process that will help shape you into the one you always intended to be.

Chapters 1 and 2 will help you remember who you truly are and step into your greater identity as a spiritual being learning to be human. Chapter 3 presents some crucial definitions and explains the seven levels of consciousness, known in Eastern philosophy as the human chakra system, we live upon as we journey from being a fragmented ego to becoming a whole and true Self. The track that we follow in our awakening is not linear. We travel at various speeds, even cycling back over the same stages sometimes in a spiraling fashion, moving deeper and deeper to integrate aspects of a truth we did not fully comprehend at the last reading. As we deepen, our Self-awareness expands. The material in this book is not something you will just read; it will change your life. In chapter 4, you'll learn about how the soul speaks to us through symbol, and the method it uses to make us whole.

Chapter 5 prepares you for your journey of further awakening by helping you clear your mind and open your heart to experiencing your deeper Self. The following 12 chapters describe the 12 Principles of Wholeness that keep us moving along our path in healthy, grace-filled ways. Each Principle describes a Life Lesson that we must learn along our way and gives some experiential ways to actually ground each Principle into daily life. The ending chapter summarizes ways to keep this process alive in your daily life and suggests how to find your true life's work.

If you wish, you can work with each Principle and its lessons and practices for a whole month to really bring them alive in your life. This process contains the transformative lessons and practices that make us whole. The Self, and its potent methods of transformation, is awakening in you. From this point forward you will start to see its magical results.

It is the worst thing when people

do not know how to escape from the old rut.

It is dreadful when they approach

new conditions with their old habits.

Just as it is impossible to open

a present-day lock with a medieval key,

likewise it is impossible for people

with old habits to unlock the door to the future.

—Agni Yoga Teachings

CHAPTER ONE

SPIRITUAL BEINGS LEARNING TO BE HUMAN

May the earnestness of all your egos
become the Joy of our one Soul!

—Djwhal Khul

The Identity Shift That Changes You Forever

All along, we've been programmed to believe that we are mere human beings—and damaged ones at that—trying hard to become spiritual, and rarely making it. You are *not* a human being trying to be spiritual; you are a spiritual being learning to be human.

This drastic identity shift is transformational in itself. It's a redefinition of the human being, an expanded view, from thinking of oneself as a pitiful little creature needing to be fixed or saved, to one who is an awakening soul with a sacred purpose in this human life.

This true definition of who you are calls you to step out of any kind of pseudo-identity you've been believing you are, and to remember your highest intentions. You are not "the addict," "the victim," "the codependent"—or any other sub-self you've gotten identified with and allowed to run your life. Though you indeed may experience these conditions, they are not who you are. This is a gross misunderstanding, and one that affects you greatly, since how we identify ourselves determines how we live our entire lives.

Your wake-up call sounds like this: Who am I, really? And what am I here to do? What am I doing with my life? Am I on track or have I gotten lost? And if I have gotten lost, am I willing to come back to my Self?

The Self Is Both Your Origin and Your Completion

The Self is consciousness—it's who you truly are—an archetypal Human made of both spirit and matter. The Self manifests as the people we are each designed to be. As the combined entity born of the marriage of your soul and personality, the Self can think clearly beyond all the twists and turns and foggy mistakes we've made in our lives. The Self can do this because it isn't just temporal and human; it is also eternal and divine. It is always aware of the bigger picture and reminds you that you are here to mature in your human form and express your unique talents in this world as Spirit in action.

Now, you may be wondering who are you if you're not being your true Self. It may not have occurred to you before, but there is a whole committee of imposters living in your psyche who jump at every opportunity to pretend they are you. These subpersonalities, which will be explored in more depth in chapter 2, must be accessed and exposed, then positively integrated into your personality if you are ever to experience wholeness. Once made conscious and named, these little partial selves will never again have the power to block you from being who you came here to be.

Your authentic Self is a *soul-infused personality.* When you are living as your true Self, you are a being whose healthy ego has taken a backseat to the soul. Your soul then drives your motivations and behavior. Your true nature is never lost in moments of delusion, nor is it found in a moment of enlightenment, either. Your Self just is. It is without time or space and has no extremism, nor any ignorance. It depends on nothing and is attached to nothing. Your true nature shines through from within when a subpersonality does not block it. Your Self is all-pervading, radiant beauty and absolute reality—the rarest of jewels beyond all price. We are each a unique statement of the one archetypal Self. The Buddhists teach that the Self is never destroyed by earth, water, air, or fire. It is the "divine spark" or nucleus from whence we as humans spring, our root consciousness that causes us to be.

So let me ask you now: Are you willing to let your Self take over the helm and guide your life? Surely, you don't prefer the hard lessons that come from living as a pseudo-self like "the addict," "the victim," or the one who, as an excuse for harmful behavior, emphatically proclaims: "Well, that's just who I am." Consciously, or unconsciously, you choose who will be the one who runs your life.

Your Spirituality Is a Fact

Thanks to the work of consciousness explorers such as Dr. Carl Jung, we now know that spirituality is not a goal. It is not the result of prayer or meditation. Spirituality is not a treatment outcome. It is not something that we earn by good works. Spirituality is our essence.

"Spirituality" is the *dynamic internal force* that propels us toward becoming more pure-hearted and whole. "Being spiritual" refers to your authentic Self's natural state. The Self's merciless striving toward wholeness keeps us unfolding into our full expression. We are blossoming into our greater story, the one that inspires us to rise to our higher purpose here: to bring spirit into this earthly life. It is not merely a religious proposition to say that we are spiritual beings. It is a universal understanding today, even scientifically.[4]

Subatomic physicists tell us that the center of every human atom is light. Brain researchers say our brains function like a hologram, that we already have the entire cosmos in our minds. Jungian analysts say the Self is embedded as an archetype within the collective unconscious mind. Conventional religion says, "I and the Father are one," and "the kingdom of God is within." And Twelve Step programs call for alignment with a Higher Power, defining recovery as a spiritual path.

Yet even with all this validation for our true nature, it is obvious that we have not fully awakened to the implications of our spiritual identity *as fact*. This recognition of our intrinsic nature as spiritual has not had the cultural or psychological impact it will eventually have. We still behave, think and plan programs as though we are mere egos needing to be fixed—or worse, medicated and dependent on experts for our life.

Perhaps we are trapped by our own intellects that are rapidly becoming too small to contain us anymore! If both scientists and spiritual guides tell us something has been proved and we are still not living it, isn't this an ethical problem for us?

Our next obvious step toward full recovery from anything in life that is not fulfilling is to merge what we know from psychological and spiritual principles that will access the *whole* Self, both our human personalities and our souls. We need to help each other find our own strengths and inner healer, and adopt a worldview that reminds us that we each have something unique to offer the world. To recover from our misguided ways, we all need to believe in *ourselves,* standing tall with the dignity of knowing that we have a valuable, creative life to live.

We are already seasoned in the workings of psychotherapy, in well-accepted family-of-origin work. The self-help movement continues to boom. And many addiction recovery programs rest on the premise that a spiritual awakening is essential to a transformed life. So the stage is set for this holistic Spirit-driven approach to enter the world of mainstream thought and acceptance—and this begins with you.

Stepping into Your Greater Identity

Being consciousness itself, your Self is already aware of the greater story that's unfolding in your life. Remember, it can transcend time and space. It is never born and never dies, so it never lives in fear of anything at all. It's the pure blueprint carrying all the natural qualities of all that you are intended to be.

The mind of your authentic Self functions as a nonjudgmental Observer who can think clearly beyond all the twists and turns you travel in your ordinary life. We're not taught much about this inner Self who holds the vision, even in the midst of your wildest conflicts and panicky outbursts. Its motivations are always pure and harmless. This observing Self is always there, though we often do not utilize it. Its function is to remind you to "lift up and out" and see your greater reality anytime you get too caught up in a personal life predicament.

I am what's termed "a clinical near-deather," having died a few minutes during a health crisis when I was twenty-nine. When out of body during my "death," I heard me saying to myself, "Now you're dead. Look at this." *It was the same consciousness that is speaking to you right now.* Then as I was drifting away, I thought of my eight-year-old son who was a juvenile diabetic and was going to be motherless. Once I thought of him, I felt the pang of his heart and was magically back in my body, aware that my doctor was there, saving my life. I tell you this so you will know it's true that our consciousness never dies. On some level, we go on and on, no matter where we are.

Wouldn't it be nice if we could live constantly in the identity of this eternal, sacred Self that we already are—and allow it to mature us into the being whom we came here to be? It nearly always takes some kind of drastic crisis for us to get the point. We spend much of our time looking back at who we've been. But unfortunately, when we see ourselves through a rearview mirror, we lose touch with the Self who is looking right through our eyes, the one who lives in the eternal Now.

CHAPTER TWO

YOU ARE NOT YOUR EGO

Your ego is a marvelous fiction . . . a false mirror . . .
a novel written by ourselves about ourselves.
And the very first step on the Quest is to
disentangle ourselves from its seductions.

—Yatri (Unknown Man)

The Ego's Job Description

You *have* an ego. But you are not your ego. Though it is indeed the ego that gets us in so much trouble, it's dangerous to ever think we are to just kill it off. The ego is the director of our personality. When we took human form, the ego was designed specifically to maneuver us safely through this concrete reality and to remind us

9

we must meet our basic needs. If we don't, our ego becomes shadowy and acts out unconsciously, sometimes even in animalistic, subhuman ways. As you awaken, you'll willingly take responsibility for gaining the missing qualities or understanding that you need to master whatever parts of your ego may have gotten shattered or ill-formed when you were growing up. This is called "shadow work," or more specifically, it will be "subpersonality work."[5]

We do not start out in life with a perfectly formed ego. We get wounded and misshapen as we learn to forgo our childlike ways and live in a socialized manner as human personalities. Anytime we experience painful abuse or neglect when we are young, a part of our ego splits off into a fragment of our developing personality, and a little self gets formed that we use to gratify a certain unmet need. We all know the "whiny baby" who cries to get nurtured and the "mega mouth" who yells to get attention. And as we get older, we become more subtle in creating and acting out these little sub-selves: the manipulator, the victim, the control freak, the adapter. Now, we certainly don't do this consciously; this process of ego-splitting happens through our autonomous, all-powerful unconscious mind. At some point, to be whole, we must learn to recognize these little selves in operation and make them conscious. Otherwise, they will rule, or even ruin, our lives.

Those Who Pretend They Are You

Some of those imposter selves we call "subpersonalities," you might recognize in yourself as you awaken, are these:

The Addict wants what it wants when it wants it and looks outside to get it.

The Codependent gives away its power to others and has no sense of self.

The Saboteur always makes sure you fail anytime you're about to succeed.

The Victim blames others, feels powerless, and sees perpetrators all around it.

The Critical Parent always reminds you of your faults.

The Seducer or Seductress uses manipulation and charm, and sometimes sexuality, to win others over or to feel special.

The Wounded Child can't take criticism or accept adult responsibility.

The Little Professor knows everything already and likes to tell you so.

The Eternal Youth never grows up, remains adorable and charms someone else to pay his or her way.

These are but a few of the masks our shadowy ego wears. Once made conscious and turned in a positive direction, however, they serve a valuable function in our subjective life.

Anytime you find yourself behaving in a way that is "not you," it's very important to identify who just took over your mouth, your eyes, your brain, your feelings and your behavior. A subpersonality has stepped up to the plate. So go within and see this self with your inner eye. See what costume it wears, and what role it is playing for you. Then give it a name—a humorous one is best. My husband named his impetuous self "Mr. Must Have." My children once named my bossy ways of mothering "Mafia Mom." This helps us dis-identify with them and give them compassion in a lighthearted way. They are like children masquerading as adults. And they carry a part of who we are, crying out to be healed.

A Self Divided Cannot Stand

Psychological healing goes hand-in-hand with spiritual awakening. All our little subpersonalities must heal and come into the light of compassion and acceptance so we can be an integrated personality. In fact, a healthy psyche will be the very foundation upon which any spiritual life is built. If we are split into fragments we believe are "good" and others we believe are "bad," our spiritual life won't be spiritual at all; we'll be filled with judgment and negativity while masquerading as a spiritual person. Some part of our unhealthy ego will rule us, and we can even misinterpret what it means to be spiritual. Consequently, there's no escaping this fact: Without a healthy psyche, we create a bogus spirituality and an unruly life.

Because we are made of both spirit and matter, like anything else in creation, the fundamental principles of our *whole* nature must be honored for us to thrive. If your nature is violated, like a hothouse violet in a snowstorm, you will wither and die. Both psychological and spiritual principles must be honored for you to experience your wholeness. Thus, the term *psychospiritual*.

Psychological work designed to build healthy ego skills is very good work, but without its spiritual counterpart, it will only take you so far. It still leaves us feeling that something is missing until we learn to meet our soul's higher needs as well. In a holistic approach to wellness, some people will need more psychological work to heal their past, while others may need more direct experiences of spirituality to realize they are "more than what they look like."

Transformational inner work is not a linear skill-building process; it unfolds as a series of "death/rebirth" experiences. You "die" to your old ways of being while new ways are taking form. Your identity constantly expands to include more of who you are. This is an ongoing process. When in a "death cycle," you will sometimes look as though you are digressing instead of going forward. But every "death" is followed by a "rebirth." Death and rebirth, in fact, cannot be divided; they are two parts of the same process. And it helps to remember this when parts of your life—or parts of your ego—are falling away.

Often your changes happen while you are looking the other way! People will tell you that something inside them just shifted, and the craving for that "whatever" that was tearing up their lives just magically fell away. This is the power of transformation.

Everyone is evolving. But those of you who consciously choose to grow move faster—which, frankly, is not always fun—you have entered what mystics sometimes call "the accelerated path." In this fast lane of transformation, you'll see that your soul won't allow you to stay in any kind of misalignment with Spirit for long. It is *relentless* in bringing us the lessons we require to integrate our personality. If we don't learn our lessons from the inside—through therapeutic inner work and inspired insights—we'll get a painful experience in our outer life, and we will call it Fate.

When Your Personality and Soul Marry

It is up to us to heal our wounded ego and honor its partial selves for what they need, so our personality can integrate its separate parts and then marry the soul. At some point your ego begins to tire of its predictable, stagnant, off-centered ways and starts craving something new. Your ego wants to "be high." It then calls out to the soul—not realizing it may have to die when the soul responds.

Now, the soul is light. And where does darkness go when light enters the scene? It dissolves. So it is with our ego's still unintegrated "stuff." As the soul descends into your physical life, it will first lighten your heart. Then it turns up the fire and, as the alchemists say, "cooks the ego in the waters of Spirit." You'll start to lose your hardened edges and fiercely held opinions and feel vulnerable and small as you begin to be less in charge.

The light of your soul will burn away any dross in your personality that could hold you away from compassion and self-acceptance. The soul will extract "the gold" from your personality— all the true parts of you—and will melt away the rest. It is molding you into your true design. And I need to tell you that this doesn't always feel so good. We are used to being ego-dominated and attached to the familiar, no matter how dysfunctional the familiar may be. So, at first, you might resist the surrender needed to proceed. If you can remember to "let go and let God," you'll transform into your authentic Self with much more grace. Egos do not relinquish their control so easily. And the more we kick and scream, the worse it is for us.

The ego and soul are an *antinomy*—paired opposites existing side by side. The two together make a whole Self—each having its own unique expression. Their "oppositeness" is never to combine or each would lose its true gift of expression. The best symbol I've seen for this marriage is the Chinese Yin-Yang symbol. There is a reverent honoring of each by the other, when they become united. Each completes the other.

As you become a soul-infused personality, you'll notice you become less intense, less invested in outcomes, and more relaxed in the moment. Your passion for life and sense of humor returns and you are openhearted and easy to be with. Sometimes you'll actually feel moments of bliss!

When you live your life as a soul-infused personality, you will know that all your experiences, even the most painful ones, have a sacred purpose. From this more integrated level of consciousness, we learn to forgive ourselves and each other for the mistaken turns we've made along the road.

Eventually we realize that all these little subpersonalities have been our instruments of transformation, the "fire by friction" that has perpetually pushed us forward. Anytime we start to go off-track and lose our way, we can remember to step into our true Self and come back to center.

CHAPTER THREE

PREPARATION FOR INNER WORK

At a time of crisis in any civilization certain
individuals turn from the outer world
to the inner life of the psyche. And, discovering
there is a new way of life, they return to
the outer world to form a creative minority, which
acts as a leaven for the renewal of that civilization.

—Arnold Toynbee

Your Psyche Is the Playing Field

Our psyches become the battleground where the formidable
conflicts between our spiritual souls and our ego-driven personalities play out. Our ancestors devised the institutions of human

psychology and religion to address this burdensome misalignment and hopefully help us transcend it. Unfortunately, however, we've wound up experiencing very little soul-work. Though the word *psyche* means "soul" in Greek, *psychology* has forgotten that its name means "the study of the soul." And our religions often mention the soul, but give little instruction concerning its nature.

Psychospiritual inner work offers us a way through this ego–soul conflict. When you have a direct experience of seeing that you are a spiritual being learning to be human, it melts away shame and blame, and fills you with the life-giving qualities of compassion, acceptance and forgiveness. As spiritual beings, we're fully aware that our schooling here has indeed been quite an ordeal. Doesn't everyone just naturally make mistakes when practicing anything new? Shame and blaming others have turned out to be major blocks to our growth and transformation. When we turn from the outer to the inner world, we do indeed deepen into the treasures of the human psyche and discover there a whole new way of life. We see everything about our lives through a wider lens. We become more loving and broad-minded.

Psychospirituality: Key Terms and Definitions

To prepare for your inner work, it will help to be clear on what the words *Spirit, soul, personality, ego, shadow* and *soul-infused personality* mean. There's a great deal of confusion about these very distinctive levels of your identity. People especially confuse soul with Spirit. So perhaps the following definitions will help:

Spirit is the hardest to define, as any definition we give is limiting. Words can only serve as signposts to its meaning. This is the highest, most expanded level of reality we can imagine. It is bigger than our intellects can even grasp. Spirit is the animating principle, the "breath of life." It is the Energy or Force of Creation itself. Spirit is formless, undifferentiated, abstract wholeness, the container for all potential manifestations. Spirit is the *impersonal;* it is the All. The use of the word *spiritual* implies that something is imbued with creative force or movement of Spirit.

Correlations with the concept *Spirit,* are: God, the All, Deity, the Universe, the Cosmos, the Void, the Divine, Logos, Oneness.

Soul resides in the in-between place in consciousness; it lives between Spirit and matter. Soul is the *relationship* between these two divergent realities. Whereas Spirit is impersonal, the embodied soul is personal; it's the actuating cause of the individual life. The soul is "twinned"; it can look both ways—upward to absorb Spirit's divine intentions, and down into our human ways.

Your Spiritual Soul looks upward and lives in its own archetypal dimension as the one Soul of Humanity, of which we are all a vital piece. It does not take on the human condition, nor does it ever become individualized. The Spiritual Soul gives you the power to rise up and out of any condition that becomes too painful or constricted. Always aware of our greater story with complete objectivity, the Spiritual Soul is equated with the masculine principle in us all, regardless of our gender.

The human soul, in contrast, embodies individually in every one of us and lives in our subjective life as the human psyche. The human soul, our consciousness, perceives our reality. I like to think of my soul as bringing Spirit ways to know how it feels to be human, and to humans a way to know Spirit. In other words, the soul incarnates to reveal the quality of the nature of God, which is divine Love. It ultimately reveals to you the purpose of your life and of all creation. The human soul is equated with the feminine principle in us all, regardless of our gender.

Correlations for the concept *soul* are consciousness, the child of

Father heaven and Mother earth (the Christ consciousness), the anima, the psyche, the heart. When it marries our personality, the embodied soul takes form as the archetypal Self.

The Self is the entity that comes alive in you when your soul and personality marry. It's the archetype of you as an individual expression of the Spiritual Soul; it is an embodied spiritual being who takes the form of each of our personalities. Your human-divine Self is your unique authenticity and expression of your greater life.

The soul, you see, is formless. The personality is ego-driven until united with soul. The ego drives our choices, and if we choose wholeness, we activate our true Self so it can express both aspects of our nature as one Being while living here on Earth. We bring it forth by recognizing it and empowering it to overtake our ego's limited ways.

Correlations for the concept *Self* are a soul-infused personality, the embodied soul, the marriage of your personality and soul, your center, your core nature, or root consciousness, the archetypal Human.

Personality is the name we give you and me as individual people. It's your body, the *persona* or mask you create and wear so you can participate in human society. Our personalities develop according to cultural, societal and family values, then behave according to their conditioning, until we're challenged along our spiritual path. Every personality is unique, and therefore an individual expression of Spirit. An integrated personality has a healthy body, a balanced set of emotions, and an intelligent mind that thinks realistically. When our physical, emotional and mental "bodies" work together in harmony with one another, we have an integrated personality. Personality, then, is ruled by either a healthy or a wounded ego.

Correlations for the word *personality* are persona; self, with a lowercased s; your individual physical appearance; and the body/ego.

Ego is the executor of our individual personalities. Its job is to look out for you as an individual. The guardian of our personalities, it decides what it will let into your mind as "reality"—which is why it can get so limited, egoistic or selfish, and even unkind or dangerous to others. Your ego will make up its own storylines based on its life experiences—*anything* to keep you safe or to meet your needs; it cares for no one but you. When healthy, however, it strives to make you harmless. It will serve Spirit. When unhealthy, it becomes shadow and fragments into several subpersonalities. Without an ego, we could not function here in individual bodies. Let's never confuse our ego's shadow with a healthy integrated ego.

The shadow is unconsciousness, your "dark" side. The human shadow is the underside of your ego and represents all its unhealed, immature, and unconscious parts. It will wear many costumes and act out various parts in your life's unfolding drama. Each fragment of your ego is a subpersonality created by your ego to get your needs met. In chapter 2, you can review examples of these little selves who form a committee in your psyche and enjoy taking over your life.

A soul-infused personality is who you become when your healthy ego has taken a backseat to your soul and allows your heart to drive your motivations and behavior in a soulful manner. When healthy and integrated, the ego becomes the soul's chauffeur and navigator in this material reality. The self is a soul-infused personality.

We Live on Seven Levels of Consciousness

When you turn inward to explore your nature, you'll discover how human consciousness works; you'll see that you operate on seven different levels of consciousness while living in your human body.[6] The three lower levels are your personality's normal development of a physical, emotional and mental life. The ego dominates at these levels, learning how to be in this material world as a healthy, socially acceptable person. A healthy ego is needed for us to feel good about ourselves and to function in relation to other human beings. Our ego development is a very sacred work: we can never transcend an ego we've never developed! So our spiritual development depends upon the presence of a solid, healthy ego.

These first three levels of consciousness become the foundation upon which your heart can open, which is the fourth level of consciousness. Coming from the heart is the first consciousness state beyond ego-driven, personalistic ways of being. This fourth level of consciousness brings us the ability to both feel and know what's true, and also, to have compassion for others. Your ego can lie to you, but your heart can never lie. To the heart, things just are what they are. Haven't you tried sometimes to go against your heart, and take on a job or a relationship that's not really right for you? You know how this feels; it simply doesn't work. You'll even hear yourself sometimes say, "My heart's not in it." Our unconscious mind will sabotage decisions we've made that go against our heart. We'll get ourselves fired or destroy what might look like a perfectly good relationship.

Because the heart only knows truth, an open heart serves as the bridge into the three higher levels of consciousness, our soul's life: Level five is where your creativity and active imagination come alive. Level six stirs your higher emotions that inspire you with strong feelings of compassion for humanity and a desire to serve. Then, when functioning at the highest, seventh level of consciousness, you become unified with a Power greater than yourself; you have mystical experiences of union and the pure ecstasy of knowing who you truly are. And you see that you are a vital player in a divine world drama, which gives your life a sense of sacred meaning and purpose.

When your heart is closed, these three higher levels of functioning are shut down—not because they don't exist, but because they can find no entrance into your conscious awareness. A closed heart is a dead feeling. Nothing excites you; it's hard to feel love for anyone or anything. You feel heavy, flat and empty all at once. Anytime you are feeling this way, stop and ask yourself what happened that caused you to close your heart. It's fear, usually; something or someone threatened you. Closed hearts create empty lives. So go deeper and find out what you fear.

I'm speaking of these seven levels of consciousness in a linear fashion, but we move up and down and all around on this ladder of human/divine experiencing, depending on our state of being and our life circumstances at any given time. We "anchor" more in the heart and marry the lower and higher levels when our ego needs are met and we have cleared a lot of our past.

Your innate wisdom of experience that knows how to live beyond ego, enraptured with life, must be accessed for you to ever reach fulfillment. Living solely an ego-driven life will never gratify us. When access to these higher ways of the soul's expression are lacking, we are left with what feels like an empty hole in our middle. Overeating, sexual acting out, and seeking chemical highs are among the resulting behaviors. The needs of every level must be met for us to find contentment.

Here are the needs of every level. You'll note that the fourth level of consciousness is the bridge between your ego and your soul life:

Chakra Function

Your Soul's Inner Life

7th Chakra honoring the intuition = aligning with a Higher Power

6th Chakra evoking inspiration, compassion, and a desire to serve

5th Chakra inciting the creative imagination and abstract thought

---

4th Chakra opening the heart [the Bridge to higher consciousness]

Your Ego's Development

3rd Chakra developing sound and clear mental life

2nd Chakra developing balanced emotional = sexual = relational nature

1st Chakra meeting basic security and safety needs

Each chakra represents a distinct level of consciousness. Conventional psychotherapy focuses mostly on chakras one through three. In a psychology of wholeness, along with working on our ego's development, we are invited to focus on accessing the four higher transformational levels of consciousness.

You have the power to access the totality of your authentic Self and then live as that One. You must be centered in your Self to access your Higher Power; an unbalanced ego can't get there. The realization that your nature is both human and divine leads you to see that the transformer of your consciousness is always within you. Transformation doesn't happen on the outside of you; through the power of inner work, you create transformation from within.

CHAPTER FOUR

METHODS OF TRANSFORMATION

One should not give up, neglect, or forget for a moment his inner life, but he must learn to work in it, with it, and out of it, so that the unity of his soul may break out into all his activities.

—Meister Eckhart

Psychospiritual Processes of Inner Work

Methods of transformation are the "tools of the trade" for any kind of psychospiritual work. These are processes that access the whole Self, not just the intellect, and not just your emotions. You participate consciously and willingly in actually experiencing what's going on inside of you and take full responsibility for whatever comes up. Some of this work you can do alone through any of these methods mentioned below. But it's helpful to be with groups who attend workshops and to undergo these processes in the company of like-minded people. You feel validated for being a seeker of Self-knowledge and less alone. You also learn more this way, from hearing others' experiences.

In a transformational process, you truly become a different person *in vivo*, living in a whole new dimension of your consciousness where the old patterns that were giving you so much trouble simply do not exist. As you "die" to these old ways, you gain inner strength and the wisdom that comes from each "death."

Here are some of the processes that will transform you:

The Power of Musical Journeys. This is one of the most dramatically effective methods I know of, as music has the power to release your brain from old stuck memories and fears. And who doesn't love music? This process is a contemplative musical journeying into the psyche to travel through memory lane. The journey can be fifteen minutes or two hours, depending on your ability to create a music set that evokes memory.

The music, having no English words, is not programming the psyche with messages from outer authorities. It is a projective tool that carries the participant from aboriginal drumming and chanting, through complex, melodic pieces that remind the ego of its earth life, like movie sound tracks can do. Then the music changes to melodic music that opens the heart. Finally, you want to end a session with higher consciousness music that brings inspiration, revelations and memories of your sacred connection to Spirit.

Soul-journeying to music accesses your unconscious mind and heals past issues still needing conscious recognition and clearing. While journeying through the inner landscape to music, you will access hard-to-reach memories and patterns that are holding dysfunctional attitudes and behaviors in place. And this happens just naturally, as though the music itself is doing the work. Often, old issues heal by just passing through them as you observe them "from above." This method magically reveals the sacred significance of your life's events, your greater story. Once recognized, these integrative insights evoke forgiveness and compassion for yourself and for others who may have harmed you in the past. This process serves to remove shame and blame, the two major blocks to anyone's healing.

Music is a powerful tool of transformation, not only psychospiritually, but physically as well. It accesses cellular memories and other past physical wounding held within the body. Research shows that music carves new neural pathways through the brain where memory and emotion converge. Entraining the mind through steady drumming evokes a meditative state of consciousness, moving us beyond the intellect. Moving through various types of music, with frequency bands becoming more complex, then smoother along the journey, affords listeners a way of "phase-locking" with certain frequencies that heal or remind them of their past and awakens them to spiritual inspirations and revelations about their greater life.[7]

Music is a universal passion that speaks directly to the soul in a completely nonjudgmental fashion. The soul already knows this work! Therefore, it is immediately recognized and loved by those who experience it.

Keeping A Daily Process Journal. Starting right now, you can keep a daily journal, one small enough to carry with you wherever you go. I call this my "little book." I use it to write down anything that comes to me during the day that has emotional reactivity or feelings I need to explore. I stop, write down what's bothering me, and just allow my hand to express whatever comes. It's the actual expression itself that discharges any pent-up feelings that might want to come forth. This process will keep your psyche clear, with the added gift of helping you tie together the cause and effect of your emotional reactivity. What just happened that caused me to feel this way, you ask? Then, you answer it. This is how it works. No one needs to ever see your "little book" but you. When you complete one, you can simply toss it. It has done its job.

You can also keep what's called "a big book." This is another type of journal that accompanies your "little book" process. It's where you record sayings, quotes, revelations, dream interpretations and the like, that are meaningful for you. Artwork and symbol drawing can also be put in your big book. This one, you'll want to keep. It's your book of inspirations. I find that what accumulates in my "big book" inspires the books and articles I write. Your "big book" is filled with material that feeds your soul.

Meditation. All meditation isn't the "sitting passively in a lotus position" kind, though this is the most commonly known way. This way works for many, but not for all. Walks in nature, jogging, bike riding, working out, listening to music, or writing poetry might work best. You can find a way that works for you. Meditation is the way to go inward into a nonordinary state of consciousness where you lose a sense of time. It's a form of leaving your ordinary waking state and traveling deeper into your psyche. You'll know when you've been meditating, because you'll look at the clock and realize an hour has gone by when you thought it was only ten minutes. So find what method gives you this "time distorted, altered state" experience, and you'll realize that you've been meditating.

Guided Imagery to Music. This is a process you will have many opportunities to experience in this book. A guided imagery is included after every Principle of Wholeness, as it's one of the easiest transformational methods to use while studying a book. Just follow my instructions as you study each imagery. You may want to record the imagery and hear it back as you experience it. Choose whatever kind of music you want for background to the process as you go inward. Just be sure to use instrumental or vocal music without understandable words.

Symbolic Artwork. After a piece of inner work through music soul journeying or guided imagery, it's very effective to put something down on paper in some form of artwork that interests you. This is not about being an artist; it's about symbolic expression, which is how our soul speaks to us. Just let come whatever your hand wants to draw or paint that expresses what you just gained from your inner work. You'll be surprised at what comes out; it's as though your hand is connected to your psyche and knows things you don't consciously know. The more spontaneous and "nonthinking" you can be, the better.

The Power of Invocation. Invocation is the simple act of calling out to your inner spiritual guide, or to God, for that which you seek. It's a cocreative form of prayer, not a passive "please dear God, help me." It is a forceful command to "Send me my instruction on how to be more ..." whatever it is that you want. Your stance is one of a cocreator with the God-force, not a pitiful helpless creature who needs God to do it for you. Invocation is considered to be the prayer for the new era. We are learning to take responsibility for being responsible cocreators—with "our part" to do.

The Power of "Divine Indifference." You can learn to detach from reaction to things in life by your willingness to be indifferent to outcomes and nonessentials. This mirrors the "let go and let God" aspect of Twelve Step work. It's relinquishing control, and learning to not take things personally. It's a spiritual practice that allows people to be who they are, and life to bring what it brings, with your divine acceptance of what is. This is a potent spiritual practice, one we all benefit from, that will spare your psychic energy from getting caught up in nonessentials, or in other people's "stuff."

Radical Self-Observation, or "Seeing Double." Using your Observer Self as you walk through your days is the key for all awakening souls. Without an Observer Self intact, we can never become conscious. It's the process of watching what you do as you do it. Being a Fair Witness is your true Self's way of speaking to you: It never judges; it only points out what you're doing. "Please note that you are bawling out your daughter just now. You might want to calm down, as she is looking for an excuse to leave you." "Please note that you just turned in to your office driveway, when you were planning to drive to your neighbor's house." Your Observer Self is simply the light bulb coming on and gently tapping you on the shoulder, inviting you to stay awake and aware of Self.

While learning to use your Observer Self, if you hear yourself making a judgment or harsh self-criticism, rise above this and observe that as well. Who's talking? Just take note. This won't be your Observer Self; it will be some kind of critical authority figure, which is an ego state. Your Observer Self lives beyond ego; it is the voice of your whole Self, your embodied soul.

We can learn to live all the time while "seeing double" like this: You are the one doing the experiencing as well as the one watching it. You are both your ego and your soul. This unifies your two natures and allows them to work harmoniously to keep you awake. This true Self is the marriage of your ego and your soul.

The three most important things to observe as a daily practice are these:

• When you "go off" and stop being your true Self. (Note what subpersonality took over.)

- When you have an emotional overreaction to anything. (Note what caused this to happen.)
- When, in a relationship, you start behaving as needy, defensive, or argumentative, or find that you're trying to justify or excuse your behavior. (Note what activated this behavior in you.)

Anything you learn from any of these observations becomes data for your "little book."

Reviewing the Day. Before going to bed each night, take a few minutes to sit and reflect on your day, starting where you are now and going all the way back through the day to when you got up that morning. Notice what comes up on your inner awareness screen. These will be the events or interchanges that did not integrate—experiences that had some emotional content or something conflictual that's still floating around in your psyche unprocessed. This kind of review will help you complete anything still left unfinished, so that you can dream more deeply, and also not carry forward issues that clog your consciousness.

Once you complete the review, make a note of anything you still need to accept or forgive, and try hard to release these pent-up feelings before you go to sleep. Just making things conscious sometimes completes them. But sometimes, there's more emotional clearing work to be done. The more you can clear your psyche each evening before going to bed, the clearer you will start out each new day. This can become an ongoing evening spiritual practice.

These eight methods mentioned above, in themselves, will give you a direct experience of inner work and help you stay Self-aware and keep your psyche clear. In Appendix One, you'll find listed more examples of transformational processes that you can experience, some by yourself, others in group work. They do not happen in a linear fashion; you'll be drawn to some of them more than others at different times along your journey.

See Appendix One for a listing of other types of transformational processes that help heal the emotions and bring about spiritual transformation.

Understanding the Soul's Language of Symbols

Your soul is a very ingenious Creator, indeed an "imagineer." Your mind's image-making device is an indicator of your divinity. It is obviously a God-given power and will carry you beyond anything your ego could ever invent. To perceive the inner world through the eyes of the soul and then enter into it with expressed intent means you will fall in love with the symbolic realities, where metaphor, myth and symbol are the norm. Your inner creative imaging will awaken—which is the fifth level of consciousness—and you will begin to mold yourself into the ideal you see in your mind. Your soul's creative imagination is what brings your subjective life into greater focus. You image it. This is how your soul "thinks." Just think about it: *You can never have what you cannot imagine!* And everything you do have, you've imagined! This is how crucial the creative imagination is for us.

Symbols are messengers from a higher plane, carriers of meaning and energy. Your soul speaks to you through symbol.

To interpret the meaning of a symbol, this process will help:

1) Meet it inwardly. See it in your mind and call it by name. Examine it, draw a picture of it, look it over thoroughly. This materializes it—brings it into form through the process of recognition. Now, it will impact your psyche.

2) Respond to it. Think about it, feel ourselves as though we are

it. In this merging we will take on its qualities and come to know it.

3) Apply it to your life. You can now direct its use in this world with the meaning you give it. Make note of the insight it provides about a current life situation, or how it answers some question you've asked. Then live accordingly.

Symbols open doorways and point us to new aspects of ourselves. A symbol becomes a key to access various compartments of your Self that you may never have any other way of understanding. They are sacred messengers from the world of our greater story.

The Science of the Soul

To make it through this sacred process of becoming whole, we have to shift from dependency upon an outer-focused empirical science to the inward way of *psychic fact*. So we turn to the science of the soul. For it is only through our inner life of dreams, visions and revelations that the soul's intentions can be heard.

What exactly is a *psychic fact*, or the science of the soul? It's anything that brings an emotional response or some numinous effect upon your psyche; you actually feel it. A *psychic fact* is something that *really happens,* not in your outer life, but in your psyche, or your subjective life. A psychic fact evokes some new insight or way of feeling about something, bringing you to a whole new place within yourself. You valued a certain thing, or held some strong opinion; and now, because of some profound recognition, the whole scene changes, and what you held dear no longer seems even relevant. You also may feel a bit embarrassed at how judgmental or opinionated you've been, now that judgment is gone. Obviously if something really changes us, it's got to be thought of as real.

At times, while undergoing a process of inner work, some unseen majestic presence or mystical revelation enters your psyche and generates a strong sense of the sacred. People call these "religious experiences." These direct experiences of the sacred are the harbingers for a spiritual awakening. As a good example, AA's founder, Bill W., had a "white light" experience. Or, there is St. Peter's "burning bush." Or, scientist Francis Crick's dream of the double helix symbol that exposed the Watson-Crick architectural structure of the DNA that won them the Nobel Prize.

I once had a numinous experience that taught me there is no death, only transformation. During a musical soul-journey, I was visited by a Triangle of Light. With my inner eye, I saw Life and Death sitting opposite each other on the two bottom sides of the Triangle. As I watched, they started dancing back and forth with each other, with Life (who looked like Tinker Bell) sprinkling light on Death, until suddenly, the top of the Triangle burst into brilliant light and there appeared an unborn baby in a womb. I instantly realized that there is no death, only constant rebirth upon a higher plane.

These kinds of rich inner experiences never leave you. And no one can take them from you. They carve unforgettable pictures in your mind that teach you a whole of something all at once. These experiences affect your psyche in ways that change you forever. As you practice the guided imageries in the chapters that follow, you are very likely to have one or more of these numinous experiences.

Swiss psychologist Carl Jung said that our logic can overlook these inner truths, but can never really eliminate them, for *they are the most real thing about us!* Through the science of the soul, we start to see our outer life as the mirrored reflection of our soul's current status in its descent into matter. We stop taking the external life as the totality of our experience.

Experiment, Experience, Expression

It's not enough to merely wonder about this inner reality-in-the-making and then casually watch it fade, as dreams and inner messages are prone to do. We must each be willing to "catch hold" of these inner experiences and draw conclusions about what our soul is telling us.

Through guided imagery, musical soul-journeying, meditation, centering prayer, and other methods of going inward, we passionately engage these inner contents of our mind, and keep records of what we receive, through journaling, artwork or speaking into a recorder. In a sense, you become your own science project. Here is the formula:

- Set up the **Experiment** by choosing a method of going inward.
- **Experience** as fully as possible whatever comes spontaneously into your mind or on your inner awareness screen.
- **Express** it. Be a living piece of data, a representative of the realizations, ideals or wisdom you gained from your inner experience.

These are the "three E's" of the science of the soul. As you start to real-ize (make real) your inner life of dreams, visions, intuitive knowing, and reflections, it gets even better: You will start to recognize that you are indeed a cocreator—that the Self is a dynamic, evolutionary Being participating in its own cocreation. And we learn that there is an intrinsic spirituality felt and experienced as a *psychological fact.* Your spiritual life begins to "show" from the inside out, as if by a magic marker. Your inner and outer life are becoming one.

CHAPTER FIVE

THE PRINCIPLES OF THE SELF

You must know the whole
before you can know the part
and the highest before you can
truly understand the lowest.

—Sri Aurobindo

Turning Inward

Upon our inner landscape, in states of deep meditation and remembrance, we transcend both time and space. We can go anywhere that's ever been imagined in this universe. Inner work is both psychological and spiritual; it'll take you either backward or forward in time, depending on what your psyche decides you need at the time to help you gather up all of your Self. You can think of inner work as an active form of meditation.

When using psychospiritual methods of inner work, such as guided imagery or soul journeying to music, your consciousness can travel backward in time to recall lost parts of yourself, or to even go further back and connect with your ancestral lineage. Conversely, you may travel forward in time and gain an under-standing through direct experience of some potential you've not yet unleashed, or you might receive a message from your soul about your emerging life's work. Trekking back through your biog-raphy is psychological work. Gaining revelations concerning your potential unfolding or your life's purpose is spiritual work. Both processes are sacred. Lost parts and unused potential hold us pris-oner or limit our soul's expression. Either way you go, you will expand into more wholeness.

Until all is made conscious and owned—not "fixed," just owned and accepted for whatever it is or was—we are still in need of more healing. *Your psyche is not seeking perfection; it is seeking completion.* This inner journey to your Source demands that every aspect of your unconscious mind becomes fully conscious. Some issues and repressed material that rise up to be seen will integrate quite easily, while some can create fear and defensiveness. Frankly, it's resistance to the process that creates most of the pain.

Once you recognize something, experience it fully, and own it truly *for what it is,* it releases on its own. You've made it con-scious. Your psyche will now be free of the charge around this issue that was causing you to react in some way. Now made known, this issue will no longer command your attention or take up any of your psychic energy. This is how emotional healing hap-pens. This is the importance of inner work.

For you who are new to inner work, all this may sound a bit

"weird." For you experienced travelers, you'll feel that I am simply describing in words what you already know. Inner work is the process of subjectively living through all the trials and jubilations of Self-realization. For you newcomers to this process, you'll be fascinated at the treasures buried in your psyche's vast inner landscape. And believe me, a meeting with your true Self is always quite a shock: you are so much more vast and wondrous than you'd ever imagined! But until you know your Self from your own direct experience, the tendency is to look outside to find something to complete you.

Living Truth

The 12 Principles you're about to study and enter into experientially are not simply intellectual ideas, nor are they drawn from any one of the world's great philosophies or religious paths. They are living truth. They are each a "seed thought" that will germinate in your mind as an inspired idea and will blossom anytime you need one of them to guide you. They have been distilled from the inner work of many who found them to be the guiding principles that keep us moving toward wholeness in a positive and healthy fashion. Anytime we violate one of the Principles, we will fall into fragmentation and head "off the mark."

There is a Life Lesson and an experiential imagery exercise accompanying each of these Self Principles. Guided imagery has been shown to access cellular memory and modify our neural programming. It's a process that is capable of healing both physical and emotional ailments. The exercises contained with each Principle invite you to experiment with deep reflection on what each imagery is designed to bring you. These exercises may cause physical sensations, or unleash blocked emotion. They can put you in a contemplative state where you'll see your bigger story or gain more understanding of some issue or pattern in your life. When we can experience the bigger picture of anything happening in our biographical lives, it is a healing experience; we no longer take it so personally.

We are always filtering, storing, learning, remembering or repressing material that comes into our minds. The brain lights up in exactly the same neural patterning when experiencing a real experience or a memory; the physical brain cannot tell the difference in something real or something envisioned. This is why guided imagery and energy-based therapies are so powerful in one's healing process.

Various types of intention training, such as visualization exercises, help bring pertinent information to a level of self-awareness. But we may not ever know intellectually how something changes; your unconscious mind is all-powerful, all-knowing and can be harnessed for healing or change without the conscious mind ever figuring out what happened.[8]

Each of the Principles you will study here corrects a painful illusion concerning life or the Self you may have carried since you were a child. These illusions or emotional reactions may have protected you in some way in the past; that is why you retain them. The soul's timing must be right and your personality receptive for a new truth or new way of feeling to penetrate your ego's defenses. If something you read does not speak to you, just let it pass on by. It may not be important for you now.

If a particular Principle does speak to you, it's probably helping you complete a life lesson that is up for you right now. The same may be true if you experience a strong resistance to one of them. Perhaps the message that repels you is pointing to an aspect of your shadow, something you'd rather not face. Or it could be

pointing to an emotional addiction you are carrying unconsciously. So take note if you react strongly to any of the Life
Lessons presented here. See if you can work past your resistance
and get to the underlying truth of your strong emotional reaction.
All that is offered here is designed to enhance your well-being.

Surrender the Mind to Love

To be willing to grow and change, your mind has to open and
validate your quest. Your mind is an incredible instrument. It serves
as a filter between your conscious and unconscious life, defining
what is acceptable and real. If it happens to be filled with false
ideas, limitations, or fears about personal inner work, it will create
a mental boundary and you can get stuck in nongrowth. Your mind
has the power to hold you imprisoned by how it has shaped
reality. As mentioned previously, modern physicists and human
consciousness research tell us that thought creates reality. So, you
may need to soften any rigidly held mental limitations to embrace
the following Principles of Wholeness.

Your mind must give permission for your heart to open. I know
many people who fear their feelings and thereby live with a closed
heart filled to the brim with unprocessed emotions. There is no
better way to open your mind to truth than to surrender your
mind to Divine Love. You can affirm this anytime—even right now:

I am willing to release any rigidly held dogma or
unexamined beliefs and allow the truth
of my being to be revealed to me.

Now, here's another mental limitation: If you do not accept the
fact that deep change is truly a possibility for you, you won't enter

into any necessary inner work wholeheartedly. Even if you don't quite believe it yet, the act of affirming this over and over will begin to reshape your thought processes.

A Note on Practicing The Guided Imageries

For the best results in doing the guided imageries offered in each chapter, you can tape your own voice reading each imagery, then find a quiet place to go inward and hear the instructions coming from your own Self. Or, you can ask someone close to you to read the imagery for you. Either way will provide you the opportunity to go deeply into the meditative experience each imagery exercise is designed to bring.

You will notice there are four dots after some of the lines in each imagery. These are to be pauses for several seconds, giving your psyche time to absorb the essence of each suggested image or statement.

So now we will begin deepening into this process through the next 12 chapters with the 12 Principles of the Self that ground your awakening into your daily life. They will meet the needs of both your ego and your soul, so that no part of you is left untouched.

Here is a transformational prayer you can say every evening at the closing of the day, to keep you grounded in absolute reality:

Let reality govern my every thought
and truth be the heart of my life.
For so it must be—especially now—
and help me to do my part.

One way to work with these Principles is to take one for each month of the year, and practice it in your life for a whole month. You can study these in combination with applying your Observer Self consciousness, using your "little book" to record your reactions and observations, and then focusing each night on a daily review. In so doing, you go far in becoming all that you wish to be—in one year's time or less. Living these Principles and doing these exercises will naturally lead you to the next step: embodying your greater Self in your everyday life.

This is a rare opportunity to tune out your outside world for a while now and turn inward to get to know your Self. You've been hearing a lot about the truth of your being. Now it's time to feel your way into it.

> Work of the eye is done; now go
> and do heart work.
>
> —Rainer Maria Rilke

CHAPTER SIX

THE FIRST SELF PRINCIPLE
"We are both human and divine"

There is neither spirit nor matter (separately)
in the world; the stuff of the universe
is spirit-matter. No other substance
than this could produce the human molecule.

—Pierre Tielhard de Chardin

We humans are a hybrid species made of both spirit and matter. Mystics throughout the ages have always known this. And today, scientists are catching up. Realizing that you are both human and divine is the act of Self-remembrance that lays the founding principle for everything you aspire to do and be. This new evolutionary impulse is awakening in our psyches now, demanding to be known. No longer do we see ourselves as mere egos needing to be fixed; we are uncovering a deeper truth of our being, realizing (making real) that we are both human and divine. When you honor only one side of your nature, you'll diminish both halves and will walk around with that empty feeling that something is missing. Both sides of our nature are to be made legitimate now, or we will never feel whole.

We ultimately learn from traveling the path of awakening that being "only human" doesn't satisfy our soul. It's very tempting to try and be "just spiritual" and rise above our human problems, but this doesn't work, either. We can never transcend anything we've not healed and integrated in our personal life. Our problems will continue to show up until we are truly done with them. In soul work, there can be no pretense. What is *is*.

For you who are recovering from addiction or religious abuse, it's crucial that you realize that this human existence with its fiery nature and juicy passions is as much a part of your sacred being as your spiritual longings and urges toward selfless service. Rejecting our God-given humanness, or labeling its natural desires as selfish or evil, negates the sacred purpose of being human. The shame created from this way of thinking is why, I believe, addiction and self-destructive behaviors are so rampant in our American culture.

We are made to enter fully into human life, so we can learn its nature. This is what Spirit is doing here—clothing itself in physical sentience so it can spiritualize the earthly existence here. If we see being human as beneath us, or improper in any manner, then we have to say that God made a mistake in creating the entire human kingdom.

Owning Both Sides of Ourselves

Paradoxically, while being human has so often been held in contempt, it has not been okay to own our divine side, either. This is usually considered arrogant or downright blasphemous. How can we ever say that we are already spiritual? Isn't this something we are supposed to forever long to be? Yet, the Bible says we are made in God's image, that we are God's offspring. In Psalms 82:6 and John 10:34, it even says "ye are gods." Yet, in this culture, we're constantly given a stern ultimatum to see Jesus as the only Son of God. And unfortunately, this lets us off the hook in accepting our sacred duty as God's representatives here as well. So, we're sinful in either direction—as human or divine. Is it any wonder, then, that we have trouble accepting who we are when our whole nature has been vilified?

When we are just naturally being ourselves, our little egos crave ascendance into the high and holy, while our soul longs to descend into the physical world to experience earthly pleasures. Our inborn drive toward transcendence and our natural yearning for the pleasures of the flesh are attempting to live within us side by side. And with all this mistaken understanding about our nature, many people get hooked on drugs, sex, passionate fighting, or other ways of gratifying our fiery nature. This dualistic pull toward ascent and descent is the sacred dance of life. As both an ego and a soul, we can learn to live within this tension by honoring both these natural urges.

When feeling the need to be spiritual, you are called to turn inward. You can go into meditation or quiet prayer or reflection, take quiet walks in nature, and cultivate your daily spiritual life through focused self-observation. When you are drawn to be more outgoing and practical, you can throw yourself into the human life. You can focus on living a healthy social life—being successful at your job, earning a good living, eating delicious food, having a good sex life, and all the human rewards that gratify a balanced ego. In the Gospel of Thomas, Jesus said, "When you make the two one, the inside like the outside and the outside like the inside; and the upper like the lower . . . then you will enter the kingdom."

The soul is your mediator between Spirit and matter, which means that your soul is in touch with both Spirit's ways and your oh-so-human ways of being. When recognized and invited in, our abstract, ethereal soul enters into our life experiences and enhances the sensual with the lightness of reverence, joy, deep compassion, and fulfillment. When the soul awakens in a human personality, a moment of wholeness is experienced: we are fully human and fully spiritual all at once. Your Self, who lives your greater story, sees purpose in all your endeavors. So no moment is lost, nor is it ever boring. This is the greatest "high" of all.

Spirit, soul, and body are one—like vapor, water, and ice! There can be no separation. The body is concretized spirit. Learning to stand tall in your earthly/heavenly nature is the key to being centered and vitally alive in this complex world. It is such a relief to the soul for us to remember that we are divine beings wrapped in human skin with the sacred purpose of becoming fully realized human beings. Lightheartedness and an intense sense of sacred meaning become the paradoxical experience of your life.

THE LIFE LESSON
Being Who You Were Born to Be

The life lesson for this first principle is practicing how your two natures can learn to exist in one body, to harmonize and spiritual-ize your life. No longer split between feeling one part of you is good and the other bad, you learn a great spiritual law: how to dis-solve either/or thinking. This is truly what makes us sick. Remember, addiction is a disease of extremes and fanatical ways of polarizing ourselves into right/wrong, sinful/spiritual. A person divided cannot stand.

So, first, let's look at your attitude toward your human side. Ask yourself:

- Am I ashamed of my humanness?
- Does my religion subtly or not so subtly make me feel this way?
- Do I go about trying to be "just spiritual"? Am I a hypocrite?
- Am I smearing a superficial layer of positive thinking over a whole bunch of negative feelings about who I believe I am?
- When my human appetites get stirred, do I go into denial and act them out unconsciously—by overeating, drinking or drugging, or chasing after sexual pursuits? If so, what am I really hungry for?
- Do I overuse my human side to avoid believing in spirituality?
- Does a fear of losing my humanness and all its pleasures keep me from having a spiritual path?

Though spiritual factors do operate behind all the functions of the lower world, they should never stop us from being fully engaged in this earthly life, nor should we ever see being human as "beneath us" in any manner. This violates our sacred reason for being born in human flesh.

Now, it's true that you may have become addicted to some of the enticing pleasures here on Earth. And if so, you must be the one to take responsibility for dropping this extremist way of living if you truly desire to move into balance. We all have our shadow dance to do with these distortions, dangers and demons that have troubled our lives. They are unfortunately part of the human condition until all is eventually made conscious, used for good, and seen as sacred.

The Significance of Addictions

People whose life lessons pour through the vessel called "addiction" are the muses of the soul. When your passions are turned in the right direction, you bring us inspiration. You are prone to turn toward the inner life with enthusiasm and to discover your psyche's greatest secret: that you already have within you all you need to be whole.

So why not accept this about ourselves as well as about others, instead of sitting in judgment or in shame? How else does a soul learn to be human without needing some practice and making false moves? Practice, with no judgment, is a key to our becoming whole. Otherwise, we get stuck in shame-based behaviors and in blaming others. These cul-de-sacs lead nowhere.

All compulsive or addictive needs we have are grounded in an emotional addiction at the root. So be sure you make conscious the emotional feeling you have every time one of these addictive behaviors or compulsive needs pops up. When you note the emotion you always have whenever this need is present, practice doing something else besides your usual emotional reaction. You want to "re-groove" your brain into some new neural pathway. And this requires repetitive practice of the new behavior. At first, you won't feel like doing it differently, but do it anyway!

What Is Your Attitude Toward Spirituality?

Now, let's explore your attitude toward your spirituality. Ask yourself:

- Do I confuse spirituality with religion?
- Am I a product of religious abuse—having been punished by authority figures "in the name of God"?

- What is my definition of "being spiritual"?
- Is my spirituality or religion something I "lay on" others as the only way?
- Am I arrogant in thinking I'm more spiritual than others?
- Do I overemphasize my spiritual life and put down being human as bad or sinful?
- Is it important for people to see me as "spiritual"?
- Is my religious life filled with unexamined belief systems?
- Do I come across as being a religious fanatic? And if so, can I admit it?
- Do I have secrets about my sexuality or sensual needs that my religion or upbringing cause me to feel guilty about?
- Do I lie to myself or have to be inauthentic in any way to "be spiritual"?
- Do I deny everything about spirituality because I've confused a negative association with a dogmatic religion?
- Do I have the right to question even parts of the Bible?

The biggest lesson on this side is to check yourself out and see if you've become "so spiritual you ain't no earthly good," as we jokingly say in Texas. Or, conversely, to see if you've denied spirituality entirely because of some form of religious abuse.

What Is "Being Spiritual"?

People who masquerade as being spiritual, when, in truth, they are simply avoiding unfinished psychological and relational business in their lives, are often more transparent than they realize. There's no way any of us can ever "play like" we are spiritual.

It's so easy to toss about spiritual platitudes, but living a spiritual life will always be a life filled with compassion, open-mindedness, and reverent concern for oneself and others. A true spiritual life is a daily practice of being observant of yourself in every moment and taking responsibility for your every way of being. Harmlessness will always be the result. Thanks to the work of consciousness explorers such as Dr. Jung, we now know that spirituality is not a goal. It is not the result of prayer or meditation. Spirituality is not a treatment outcome. It is not something that we earn by good works. Spirituality is our essence!

Anytime you start to fall into Self-forgetfulness, remembering this Principle will keep you on the mark. From this moment forward, have the courage to become the beautiful hybrid creature God made you to be: a Self who is both human and divine. It's not supernatural for people to finally come home to themselves, to gain Self-remembrance: it's the natural unfolding of our destiny.

THE PRACTICE
Stepping into Your Soul-Infused Personality
A Guided Imagery

Using your creative imagination is how you make inner mental images that create your reality. As we've now seen, your imagination is a soul power that will bridge your actual and your ideal self—carrying you from who you believe you are now, to who you wish to become.

Take a moment, then, to image your ordinary personality self, the one you've always thought you were. . . . See yourself in a current life episode, dressed as you are today, behaving in your usual fashion, and let this image become plain. . . . Now, feel your way into it. . . . Notice how you truly feel about who you are today as your human personality. . . .

Now, using your imagination, create an image of your ideal

Self—that one you hold up as perfect or complete.... (This one may be harder to access, but be patient and let it arise from your unconscious mind.) You will first sense an essence.... Then, a vague "memory" of who you truly are will begin to appear.... Notice who comes.... And feel your way into this higher Self, noticing how this image makes you feel....

Once you have these two images of yourself in your mind, let them turn toward one another and slowly come together until they merge into each other....

Now, see who you are in all your glory!

Create the image that you are standing on the earth as "a vertical rod" between heaven and earth, a representative of the link between our spiritual and our earthly natures.... There is no one or no thing between you and God.... This stance is your willingness to hold steady, with focused attention and the spiritual intention as a spiritual being living in a human body, a "demonstrator of the Divine."

To bring this Principle "home" as your natural way of being, practice daily for this month noticing how often you remember that you are both human and divine, and noting the times when you fall into Self-forgetting.

More specifically, start out each day standing up and facing the East, and saying out loud very emphatically: "I am willing to be my true Self today." After you declare this to your Higher Power, take a moment to meditate on what you just said, and anchor it in your mind.

As you go about your day, make a mental note of every time you recall your invocation. And note how many minutes or hours went by when you forgot.

If you do this practice for a whole month, it can become an ordinary way you think and feel about yourself. So give this practice a chance to settle into your consciousness your whole identity as a given fact.

The following guided imagery, done once a week for this month, will also help ground you in your true identity.

Imaging the Self You Were Born to Be

A Guided Imagery

Here's an inner-work activity that will help you embody your earthly/heavenly Self.

Find a place that has a mirror, where you can be alone and quiet for a while. Stand in front of the mirror, and close your eyes. Take a few moments to breathe evenly in and out, until you feel yourself start to relax. With your eyes still closed, bring forth a mental image of your ideal Self. . . . As you see this Self start to emerge in your mind, slowly open your eyes, look in the mirror, and focus softly on your forehead, right above your eyes. . . .

Now, see your Self looking back at you from the mirror. . . . Keep looking into the eyes of the one looking back at you until you see your Image turn into your true Self in all its glory. . . . Now, allow your identity to shift so that you become the mirrored Image looking back at you. . . .

When you feel ready, slowly close your eyes again and take some time to anchor this Self Image in your consciousness. . . . And give thanks to your Higher Power for having this right.

When you feel ready, slowly open your eyes and come back here. You might want to stay in the Silence for a while and journal this experience.

You can repeat this activity anytime you fall into Self-forgetting.

CHAPTER SEVEN

THE SECOND SELF PRINCIPLE
"The Self is greater than its conditions"

What on a lower level had led to the wildest
conflicts and panicky outbursts of emotion
now looks like a storm in the valley
seen from the mountaintop. This does
not mean that the storm is robbed of its reality,
but instead of being in it, one is above it.

—Carl Gustav Jung

Getting caught up in our life's predicaments and then losing ourselves in these conditions is the plight of every human soul. Anytime you are feeling stuck or have that awful feeling that something in your life is getting you down, you can stop right then, go within, and remember: Nothing in life can ever destroy your Self. Your being is an ever-present one that is greater than its conditions, no matter how devastating they might seem.

This Principle will help you get past your worst times. It will give you the inner strength to go through whatever kind of pain might be occurring at any time. So let this Principle sink into your consciousness, and know that it will take root and pop into your brain anytime you need it.

Your Outer Life Mirrors Your Inner World

You are *not* your divorce, or your job failure, or that current betrayal you're going through. You are not your physical illnesses, either, or your unraveling emotions during times of stress. Neither are you your most recent success or that new title you've just earned. These are all *conditions* apart from you, events, states, and roles you are passing through that are bringing you opportunities for refinement and more soul expression.

Your outer life functions like a mirror. It is never the reality, only a reflection back to you of how you are creating your life. It will reflect your belief systems, your attitude toward life, your self-image, and your perceptions of what's going on. There are so many ways to see it all, so many attitudes to have. You and I are responsible for our own beliefs and perceptions. It is these inner processes that are determining our outer life.

Your outer events are the chessboard upon which all the pieces of your life are placed that bring you the human experiences of pain or sorrow, joy, love or betrayal. Because of how you think and the choices you have made, you have taken on particular situations and relationships. These circumstances, which attracted you, are specifically designed to help you come back to love.

Once we get hooked in a life circumstance, though, we so easily forget how to free up from these entanglements. Yet here's the bottom line: all that we learn here from our conditions are lessons in love. Our confusion about what love is and what it is not, however, is the key element in our advancement toward harmonious living with others. Your Self wants only love. As love, it seeks its own nature. Who you believe you are is reflected back to you, projected onto the world.

Reflect on How You Are Defining Yourself

You may want to stop a moment now and recall those favorite, often-used stories or self-statements by which you define yourself, and the plots in which you are encased as the main character. Then, go deep within and see if you can access your basic feeling state about yourself—what you feel you're actually capable of or not, or how wounded or inept you believe you are. Now see if you can step outside of all this and look at how you've created yourself. Perhaps you've been standing in the middle of your own picture, not seeing who you are. Ponder this for a few moments before going on.

Your psyche is not looking for perfection—it only wants completion! So it will bring to you the same painful experience over and over until you get the point of how to be loving, nonattached, and broadminded in any situation. The names and geography may change, but until we root out the core issue holding the dysfunction in place, the issue will remain unhealed. Once you get the sacred significance of a certain heartache or relationship breakup, you will see the lesson clearly, and then, like magic, that issue will disappear from your life. Why? Because you no longer need it.

It is your ego who gets "hooked" by the circumstances in life—that become the conditions that will, hopefully, refine it. When you are willing to be dead honest with yourself, you'll see that your ego gets hooked through pride—needing to be right, getting its feelings hurt, feeling entitled, things like this. Each human experience we undergo brings our ego into more alignment with the truth of our being—*if* we are willing to become conscious and learn from these experiences. Anytime we catch ourselves acting out of some needy ego stance, we can stop and decide what quality or skill we need to counteract this unwanted way of behaving. Through a constant willingness to remain conscious moment by moment of how we are behaving, we can shift our familiar ways of reacting, and learn to meet our ego's needs through the positive qualities hidden underneath the shadow's ways of being. For example, if you are possessive, you're probably capable of deep commitment. If your feelings are easily hurt, you may be a very compassionate person.

You Are Spirit-in-Action

The will of your true Self is spirit-in-action, designed to bring spirit into all your human experience. Aligning your personal will with your highest spiritual intentions is a fascinating process that makes for a rich ongoing daily spiritual practice. As cocreators who work hand in hand with our Creator to materialize spirit in this world, we are remembering that we have "our part" to do in unfolding the divine Plan for humanity. When you feel trapped by your conditions and go unconscious, you are failing to spiritualize what is happening to you. To make something spiritual, go into your "underside," examine all the crisscrossed threads that are creating the situation, then make a decision to charge the pattern with a sacred meaning and a high purpose in your life. And realize you may even be helping humanity as a whole by doing this. The things we experience in life are never "just personal." Anytime you heal and make sacred some issue that has troubled your life, you are bringing more light into humanity's one collective psyche, thereby helping all who have a similar wound.

If we can remember that we came here as spiritual beings to learn how to be human (Principle One), we will never confuse what's happening to us with who we are. Instead, we intensely involve ourselves in life, even in the painful times, with the questions: "What lesson is there here for me?" "What is my soul's intention in this situation?" This places us upon a higher rung of our evolutionary ladder. We can learn to see things from above the storm while passing right through them. This way of living works beautifully for passionate souls. It gives intense pleasure to work toward seeing the sacred meaning to otherwise rather mundane experiences. It makes us feel connected to our Source. We can fall in love with the journey itself when we stop letting our conditions define us.

No matter how chained to the rock you may feel yourself to be in any situation, the divine Spark in you is steadily moving you toward your full unfolding. While here in human form, we learn best from our concrete physical experiences. Remember "the three Es" of how your soul sets up its scientific experiment to know itself in human form: experiment, experience, expression.

You are the one who sets up the *experiment* by choosing a method of learning. You then *experience* the lesson as fully as possible so you can learn it all the way through. Once learned, you become the *expression,* a living piece of data of the wisdom gained from the experience. You are never just the experiencer. The You who inhabits your physical body is consciousness itself.

THE LIFE LESSON
Learning Through Symbol or Symptom

If this Principle is speaking to you, some tough lesson in your outer life may have come upon you like fate. So you're probably needing to learn one of two things: remembering to enter fully into whatever feelings you may be avoiding, so you can complete this experience, or needing to surrender some ego stance and detach from some situation or relationship that has lost its spirit.

There are two ways to learn our lessons. We can travel the "high road" and learn through *symbol,* which is the inner way. Or we can travel the "low road" and learn through *symptom,* which is the outer way. If you can get the symbolic meaning of a troublesome condition, the pattern you're living through will be revealed. Then you won't have to act it out as a symptom of disease or dysfunction in your outer world. This is the gift of inner work. If we don't learn something through inner work, however, it will come at us from the outside as some uncontrollable disaster we're required to deal with.

Here's an example: You have a new boss, someone you don't really even know. Yet, you already can't stand him and resist doing every job he assigns you. And the relationship is in jeopardy. If you will go inward and discover "When have I felt this way before? Who does he remind me of?" you'll realize that this is some unfinished business with your father. You will see you're still trapped in how you've always felt about yourself in relation to your dad. Symbolically, this new boss is giving you the opportunity to step out of that "father complex" and see your boss in reality.

With this understanding, you may still have the feelings of resistance to your boss, but you won't need to act them out. Instead, you'll take the "high road" and journal your feelings, or discuss them with a friend or therapist. At work you'll be conscious that this man is currently your teacher. If you take the "low road" and act out this error in perception, getting fired may be the outer symptom, your fate. Either way, through symbol or symptom, we learn. But I'd sure rather take the "high road," wouldn't you?

When you hear yourself say "I don't like seeing me act this way," you must realize you are two selves. The one who is acting out, and the one who doesn't like seeing it! Which one would you rather be? All troublesome ways of behaving are coming through an imposter self. Keeping ourselves clear inside saves us from emotional and physical dis-ease. The ideal would be to remain so transparent that the winds of our circumstances can flow right through us with nothing to stick to.

Symptoms Are Reminders to Turn Inward

So, anytime something is worrying you a lot, see it as an opportunity to go inward and find the symbolic meaning of what's really bothering you. There is an emotional attachment you always feel when this particular person or situation comes upon your awareness screen. It means the symbolic significance of what this reaction is trying to defend has never been accessed, made conscious and healed. Be willing to clear it out. Just realize that this upset feeling means you are "cooking," which is the sacred alchemical process the soul brings to us when making us into someone new. It is felt as a churning or a thud in your heart. When you're "in a stew," just know that you are in the very act of transformation itself. The Self, your soul, is burning away some ego mistake or illusion and reformulating you.

All issues in life are relationship issues. Some are with people, some are with your career or a particular "something," like alcohol or shopping, you've become addicted to. You can apply the following questions to a relationship of any kind that may be troubling you:

- Is this a pattern I've experienced at other times in my life? If so, what is the lesson I'm not getting?
- What is the emotional addiction underlying the feelings I have in this relationship? How do I always react when my feelings are set off?
- Am I honoring my authentic Self by being in this relationship?
- What is this (whatever) giving me that I believe I don't already have in myself?
- Does this relationship still have soul, or is it just my ego that won't let go?
- Has the purpose of this relationship been met, and expired? If so, am I willing to kindly walk away?
- What do I represent for this other person? And, what does he or she represent for me?
- What about me drew this type of person (or whatever) to me?
- If it's a primary relationship, ask yourself this: When I'm just naturally being myself and he or she is just naturally being him or herself, do we respect and honor each other just as we are? If not, why not?
- Am I spending my energy trying to change this person rather than looking at my own part in this?
- Is this person trying to tell me something I'm not hearing?
- Are we just in the wrong roles with each other and our relationship needs redefinition?
- What is this experience teaching me about love?

This kind of self-inquiry requires radical self-honesty and a willingness to own your part in whatever disturbance is going on. Blaming others is often projection, which is a nongrowth choice.

Remind yourself that you are the one who set up this experience. And you are the one experiencing it. So identify with that one who set it up if you can—this is your true Self—and see if you can lighten up and stop taking things so personally.

Sometimes this mantra helps: "No resistance. No resistance. Let it be." Another one that helps me a lot when I say it to myself is, "This, too, shall pass."

THE PRACTICE
Using Your "Little Book"

During this month, you will learn a lot about how you react in troublesome situations by observing which kinds of situations "hook" your emotions, how you behave when you are "hooked" and how you overcome the attachment. Remember what feeling "hooked" feels like: It will be a churning in your gut or a pressure in your chest, making you feel anxious and restless with a compulsive urge to get something explained or eased. You're in process—you're "cooking." Use your Observer Self to notice which subpersonality gets activated when you feel a certain way.

Use your "little book" to express the feelings when they appear, and listen to what the feelings have to say. Do this faithfully every day this month to ground this exercise into your daily life as an ongoing practice.

Make note of the stories you tell yourself that keep your emotional reactions going full blast. There will always be a personal "little story" (my father always criticized me), and then an impersonal "bigger story" (I've never resolved my father complex, so I have trouble with male authority) that explains the symbolic meaning of your interactions.

Following is a guided imagery that is transformational. Do it once a week this month, or as often as possible.

LIVING INTO YOUR BIGGER PICTURE

A Guided Imagery

If it's time to let go of some lingering emotional attachment now, there is a mental process that is so simple, it can easily be overlooked for the power it has to heal you. This process is: stop long enough to focus inward, call out for help from your Self, and remember "the bigger picture."

Find a quiet place where you can do some inner work. Close your eyes, and reflect on the current predicament in your life that is giving you grief. Take the time to really let this situation come in on you—see it in your mind, and enter into it, fully absorbing how this circumstance is making you feel. . . .

Now, as if by magic, lift up and out of this scenario, as though you are rising up out of your conditions and into the sky, viewing it all now from above. . . . From this higher station, see what it is that's *really* going on; see the bigger picture. . . .

See the lesson, the context in which this situation is occurring. Perhaps there's a pattern. . . .

See the image back in behind this scene that is holding it all in place? Where did you learn to have this response to this particular kind of situation? Reflect on your past for a while and gather up this pattern. . . .

Now, see yourself reentering the scene you'd risen above, and imagine resolving the situation in your new way. . . .

Come back to this reality and take some time to reflect.

Never forget for a moment the power of your authentic Self. It can always ease your suffering and bring you back to the reality of any situation. Your inner Self is your Beloved, the soul. It's good if we can all help one another remember this and encourage this new evolutionary impulse. Following the tendencies of egoism alone, where you only think of yourself, no longer satisfies our hungry souls.

CHAPTER EIGHT

THE THIRD SELF PRINCIPLE

"Whatever you say 'I am' to, you become"

The words "I am" are potent words;
be careful what you hitch them to.
The thing you're claiming has a way
of reaching back and claiming you.

—A. L. Kitselman

The words "I Am" emanate from the Divine. They carry the power of manifestation. This means that whatever you say "I am" to, if it is powered by an emotional charge, will become your reality. Spiritual teachings both East and West hold these two words in reverence at the highest level.

We must never say "I am" to anything less than who we truly wish to be, for it will be mirrored right back to us. To say I am to an affliction or condition—such as "I am angry," or "I am just beaten down by life"—will manifest the very thing you'd hoped to never have to deal with. And here's why: The "I" in you does not behave like a person; it is only an energy matrix that contains all the qualities of being human. The "I" is pure consciousness. It will take the form of whatever you choose to call yourself at any given time.

There is a big difference between the words "I am" and "I have." "I am" claims you, while the "I have" statements indicate something you possess. Common expressions such as "I am upset," or "I am a failure" are how we speak ordinarily. We often don't realize this, but these statements are determining our lives. We misuse language out of our ignorance about how human consciousness works. Then, because we hang out in these mistaken identities, it's hard to ever get past them. No wonder the relapse rates in addiction recovery soar as high as 90 percent.[9] How many times have I heard someone in recovery say, "I just can't help it; I am a hopeless alcoholic"?

All statements that identify us do not begin with "I am." Some are more subtle. If you say "Nothing excites me," you are really saying "I am bored with life." The thinking that's creating that reality is clearly there. It's pretty harmless to say things like "I am going to the grocery store." Or, "I am late for the party." These do not define us. Yet, you'll notice that when you make these statements, they do indeed manifest. You *do* go grocery shopping. You *are* late for the party.

The point here is this: "I am" statements are the cosmic law of manifestation at work; they create who you are. What you verbalize is a declaration of what's in your mind. And thought is creative.

When to Say "I Am" Versus "I Have"

I know I'm hitting a sacred cow in the face when I suggest saying "I am an alcoholic" might best be changed to "I have

READER/CUSTOMER CARE SURVEY

HEFG

We care about your opinions! Please take a moment to fill out our online Reader Survey at **http://survey.hcibooks.com.**
As a **"THANK YOU"** you will receive a **VALUABLE INSTANT COUPON** towards future book purchases as well as a **SPECIAL GIFT** available
only online! Or, you may mail this card back to us and we will send you a copy of our exciting catalog with your valuable coupon inside.
(PLEASE PRINT IN ALL CAPS)

First Name _____ MI. _____ Last Name _____

Address _____

State _____ Zip _____ Email _____ City _____

1. Gender
❏ Female   ❏ Male

2. Age
❏ 8 or younger
❏ 9-12   ❏ 13-16
❏ 17-20   ❏ 21-30
❏ 31+

**3. Did you receive this book as
a gift?**
❏ Yes   ❏ No

4. Annual Household Income
❏ under $25,000
❏ $25,000 - $34,999
❏ $35,000 - $49,999
❏ $50,000 - $74,999
❏ over $75,000

**5. What are the ages of the
children living in your house?**
❏ 0 - 14   ❏ 15+

6. Marital Status
❏ Single
❏ Married
❏ Divorced
❏ Widowed

**7. How did you find out about
the book?**
(please choose one)
❏ Recommendation
❏ Store Display
❏ Online
❏ Catalog/Mailing
❏ Interview/Review

**8. Where do you usually buy
books?**
(please choose one)
❏ Bookstore
❏ Online
❏ Book Club/Mail Order
❏ Price Club (Sam's Club,
   Costco's, etc.)
❏ Retail Store (Target,
   Wal-Mart, etc.)

**9. What subject do you enjoy
reading about the most?**
(please choose one)
❏ Christianity
❏ Spirituality/Inspiration
❏ Business Self-help
❏ Women's Issues
❏ Sports

**10. What attracts you most to a
book?**
(please choose one)
❏ Title
❏ Cover Design
❏ Author
❏ Content

❏ Parenting/Family
❏ Relationships
❏ Recovery/Addictions
❏ Health/Nutrition

TAPE IN MIDDLE; DO NOT STAPLE

BUSINESS REPLY MAIL
FIRST-CLASS MAIL PERMIT NO 45 DEERFIELD BEACH, FL

POSTAGE WILL BE PAID BY ADDRESSEE

Health Communications, Inc.
3201 SW 15th Street
Deerfield Beach FL 33442-9875

FOLD HERE

Comments

alcoholism." Alcoholism is a disease caused by drinking alcohol when your body can't handle it; it is not who you are. To say "I have alcoholism" instead of "I am an alcoholic" is not a form of denial, nor is it an excuse to drink again. It's simply setting the record straight about something you possess rather than something that's possessing you! It's taking your power back. When you say "I am my disease," the disease takes hold of you and you live it out. Everything in your life, then, will fall under the rubric of that diseased way of being.

To say "I am a recovering alcoholic" may be beneficial, however, during the first stage of recovery. It, in fact, may be the first identity this person has ever had. So identifying with other people who call themselves alcoholics can be a healing experience. It helps reduce the shame many with this affliction feel. But as one continues in recovery, there will come a time when this identity becomes too small to contain the person anymore. As one grows and expands, he or she will also live out of many other parts of oneself that have nothing to do with being "an alcoholic." The person may be an artist, a teacher, a quiet person, a friend. All of these are descriptive roles we play when needed. None of them are ever who we are.

You can appreciate the learning experience that any identity you adopt gives you. Your adopted identities determine what you allow to upset you, what makes you feel good about yourself, what you become attracted to and focus on, and to what you give priority in your life. For example, if you tell me that I am a bad fighter pilot, I will probably just smile. I have no investment in being a fighter pilot. However, if you say that I am a bad mother, my heart clutches and I have an emotional reaction.

So take note of what you're identified as; it will give you much information about your responses in life and why you are making them. When you are taking some identity too seriously, you're obviously "hooked." If so, you can get in touch with the need this identity is meeting for you and learn to gratify it in a healthy, harmless fashion. There are times, too, when we naturally outgrow an identity that no longer holds any meaning for us. Then, we step out of it, like a piece of outgrown clothing: we transcend it. The words we use connect us to the beliefs we have about who we are. Your outer world is nothing but a mirrored reflection of all that you believe to be reality. This is how consciousness works. This is why mythologist Joseph Campbell said we'd better have a great big story or no story at all; that it's all those little stories in the middle that cause us so much trouble. Perhaps it's better to say things like: "I am pure consciousness." "I am a child of God." "I am a soul traveling through a human life." These are our greater stories that define who we are in our wholeness. Think of the life that would manifest all around us if we'd used these whole Self definitions instead of all those little ones that minimize our lives by putting us into tiny labeled boxes. Let's ponder this for a while.

Identification and Dis-identification

Identification is the key word here. Whoever you identify as, you become. Then, it conditions your life. We never have to be stuck in a limiting identity, though, because we are capable of both *identification* and *dis-identification*. Identification, in Buddhist terms, is attachment. Dis-identification is nonattachment. Identification is "taking something on." Dis-identification is "taking something off." You step out of it and see it as something other than you. As we awaken, we learn to be good at both and to know when each is appropriate.

"The basis of all Self-realization and inner freedom is

disidentification," says the great Italian psychiatrist, Roberto Assagioli. "We will find that we are ruled by what we become identified with, and whatever we can dis-identify from, we can direct and make use of." For then it will be a higher Self who will do the directing.

We are always moving from fragmentation to wholeness on this road to Self-realization. So, anytime you've completed some stage in your life or some aspect of yourself, you are called to *dis-identify* with this limited self and move on to *re-identify* with the more expanded one you're becoming. As spiritual beings learning to be human, we are designed to live right at our growing edge. We take on; we let go; we descend into something to know it, then we ascend out of it and move on. We were never intended to hold onto anything we've outgrown. We are always releasing a lesser self for a greater one. In this manner, we make conscious our own process of Self-realization.

As you awaken, you'll want to unearth any unconscious or petri-fied attitudes or beliefs you may be carrying that could be causing you to manifest a reality not of your conscious choosing. So much of what we do in life stems from unexamined belief systems. So often, we "go on robot" and do not think at all. When caught in a negative situation, we'll hear ourselves say, "Well, this is just how I am." Shifting from unconscious to conscious living is quite a shock. When your soul awakens in your personality's life, your unconscious ways of behaving will start to hit you right in the face; you won't be able to get away with being "asleep at the wheel" any longer.

THE LIFE LESSON
Letting Go of Limitation

If reading about this Principle is attracting you, you're being called to grow beyond some part of yourself that you've outgrown. Any partial identity you become has its sacred purpose in your awakening, until you outgrow it. Then, it becomes a dead form and it will be essential for you to dis-identify.

While living within a certain limited identity, such as "the addict" or "the victim," you'll be gaining an experiential understanding of how this particular part of you behaves. This "part" will be acting out a piece of you who has an unmet need. But it's an unintegrated fragment of your ego. And because it's unintegrated, it acts out unconsciously and won't be cooperating with any other part of you. It will overtake your whole personality and behave as though it is you—like when you become your temper tantrum. Remember how that feels? You'll say and do things to the people you love the most, and later, you are aghast!

So let's take a look at some of the subpersonalities that may be creating a life you no longer want to live. See if we can identify one you may be trapped in right now, so you can move on. These are just some examples that can stir your creativity. If you're good at picturing each of these, you'll know exactly how they would behave:

- the Wounded Child
- the True Believer
- the Southern Belle
- Lover Boy
- the Perfect Son or Daughter
- Supermom
- Glamour Queen
- Pitiful Polly
- the Jock
- the Addict
- the People Pleaser
- Mr. Above It All
- Mr. Cool

Use your imagination now, and see what subpersonalities you come up with.

Once you've identified the pseudo-self you're discharging, don't take it too seriously. Just give it a humorous name, as this helps greatly with the dis-identification process. You can purge yourself of any ideas that are holding you prisoner to this limited way of knowing yourself by using your creative imagination. See yourself stepping out of it. You can start right now seeing yourself behaving as though it's gone. How might you be when you are no longer ruled by this predictable way of being? Start thinking yourself into your future instead of living in your past. All transformation begins in the mind! So just be willing to let this process take hold. You've made it conscious, and that's more than half the battle.

Letting Go and Taking On

You may be one who is better at letting go than at taking on, better at dis-identifying than identifying. If so, you will tend to avoid intimacy or any demands on your feelings. Rather than engaging, your tendency is to withdraw when things start to get sticky in a personal situation. But when your focus and commitment is required, staying too removed can be an irresponsible way of relating to loved ones. Perhaps it's time for you to risk coming closer in an intimate relationship, to commit to something or someone in a very deep and meaningful way. Maybe there's an Above It All or a Mr. Cool now ready to integrate. It's easy to look "together" and nonreactive when you live your life from a distance! But it's not a very fulfilling life.

Or, the opposite lesson may be what's up for you. You may be one who becomes too invested in your relationships, with all kinds of strong feelings and obsessive involvement. You may even feel more alive when some crisis is occurring. You could have a Do Gooder subpersonality who needs to be needed to feel good about yourself. This way of living can be quite fulfilling, because you will feel needed and will do some very useful things for others. But you can get trapped in an endless string of other people's crises, and rarely take care of yourself. So now, it may be time for you to learn to get some distance from your intense relating.

Your psyche's entire journey through the human condition could be viewed as your search for your true identity. It's a process of learning to discriminate between the "me" and the "not-me," the essentials and the nonessentials, through the unrelenting process of identification and dis-identification.

THE PRACTICE
Emotional Honesty

Take a moment and go within and let yourself feel how it is for you when you are required to seriously engage in a relationship requiring emotional involvement—one where the other person wants you to be available for honest processing and intimacy. As you imagine yourself entering into this kind of relating, check out your body and see if emotions or any kind of clutched feelings are rocking around inside you near your solar plexus or your heart. And if so, just notice.

Now, go within and let yourself feel how it is for you when you remain at a distance from people and situations requiring emotional involvement and intimate self-disclosure. As you imagine yourself remaining distant or withdrawn, check out your body and see what feelings, if any, are moving around inside you. Note especially if you have no feelings, but are just thinking with your intellect.

From this self-assessment, you will know which kind of person you tend to be, either one who involves deeply—perhaps even too deeply—or one who remains at a safe distance from emotional involvement.

Whichever type you are, make a commitment to invoke the quality that will assist you in becoming more of the way you tend to avoid. If you are an involver and good at engaging with your whole Self, though sometimes feel trapped in emotionalism or too much investment in a relationship, you can invoke the quality of "divine indifference" or nonattachment. Call it down and commit to practicing this new way of being. Practice this until all lopsidedness dissolves and you become more balanced in knowing when to involve and when to remain levelheaded and nonattached.

If you are more the distance-keeping type, preferring thinking to feeling, invoke the quality of "willingness to engage" or "willingness to feel deeply." Call it down and commit to practicing this unfamiliar way of being until all lopsidedness dissipates and you are able to be both ways, with discrimination and appropriate timing.

Use this month to practice being able to both involve and disengage. And see how you come out by the end of the month. A balanced emotional body is the key.

Another simple exercise to practice this month is to listen to your self-talk and take note of what you say "I am" to. This will give you a key to the roles and identities to which you are attached. It will show you which emotional states you are claiming as well— such as, "I am a mess." "I am feeling hopeless." "I am never caught up." "I am confused."

An Exercise in Dis-identification

Whether dis-identifying with some part of yourself you no longer need, or stepping into your true Self again in a reidentification, you will need to consciously release the subpersonality holding the reins of the particular pattern that controls you. Then, the reidentification with your true Self happens naturally. From the above exercise, you will discover the nature of the subpersonality who keeps you distant and removed from feelings, or the one who overinvests in emotional relationships.

Releasing a Subpersonality

To dis-identify from a subpersonality, you can use this three-step process:

1. Observation: *I have you.* Name the part you're releasing and see it standing before you. During this stage, you will make conscious the fact that you are not this subpersonality; you are the one looking at it. So, you can truthfully dis-identify.

2. Dis-identification: *And I am not you.* As you step out of it, ask it what it needs from you, as you would ask a small child, and tell it what you need from it. Allow the dialogue to continue until you've learned all you need to from this partial self.

3. Reidentification: *I am pure consciousness; I am the Self with an impulse to act as my true Self.* This is a statement of Self-remembrance. So take some time to anchor this awareness of who you really are, feel yourself as this one from the inside out.

You can use these steps as a daily affirmation all month. With your focus and commitment, the subpersonality will drop away.

CHAPTER NINE

THE FOURTH SELF PRINCIPLE
"The human show has a sacred function"

The shadow provides us with a sparring partner,
the opponent who sharpens our skill,
by showing us what we've negated
or simply don't know yet.

—John Conger

Your shadow is all those unconscious parts of you that you con-
sider despicable and unworthy of owning. To get its way, it uses
your negative emotions, such as rage, jealousy, possessiveness, self-
pity, feelings of entitlement, defensiveness, lust, greed, and worst of
all, blame. Because we are so ashamed of this dark side of our
nature, we try to deny we even have it. It's also much easier to see
someone else's shadow than to claim our own. Your shadow is like
an immature child, and its behavior is often exaggerated and

completely unacceptable to mature and considerate adults.

Given its dark and seemingly inappropriate nature, how can we ever be willing to own this unwanted part of ourselves? How can we say your shadow has a sacred function? Wouldn't it just be better to kill it off, or at least keep it hidden and ignored? To this I must give a resounding No! This is the exact opposite of how the shadow heals. The more we deny our shadow, the bigger it gets. Your shadow is a part of your psyche whether you accept it or not. So it has no place to go when you deny it, except to lie dormant, awaiting an opportunity to burst forth. Anytime you push down feelings of anger, hurt, or any unhappy emotion, these unexpressed feelings pile into the back closets of repression in your unconscious mind. This is your shadow's storehouse. Then, when you let your guard down and you become overly frustrated, tired, or otherwise out of touch, these powerful feelings overwhelm your psyche and dump out all those feelings you've been denying in one fell swoop—beyond your ego's control.

Shadow work is the key element in any kind of recovery process. The shadow infuses us with distorted self-images and thoughts about ourselves and life. Only the Self can provide us with genuine reflection. The shadow causes us to act in ways that create catastrophe or explosions of emotionalism. When the shadow has hold of us, we can become primitive and incapable of moral judgment—literally a subhuman self. These uncomfortable parts of us must be met, accepted, understood and integrated before we can move ahead in life.

Think of your shadow as your "holy grit." It's the sandpaper in your psyche that rubs you raw until you make it conscious. Your shadow provides you with a "sparring partner, the opponent who sharpens your skill," says Jungian analyst John Conger. It reflects back to us our blind side. It never lets us get away with being "half made."

The Shadow as Projection

The shadow can act out in subtle ways as well when we project it out onto others. If your reaction to another person manifests as an extreme of either attraction or repulsion, this person is mirroring some aspect of your own shadow. Hating or falling in love with a "mirror image" like this is more common than you might think. Projection, especially, messes with our romantic life.

For instance, you'll hear people complain that every love partner they get serious about turns out to be no good for them, usually in similar ways. You've projected your own low self-esteem onto the relationship, and thereby sabotaged it. Or, some people constantly mistake an ordinary attraction with finding a one and only "twin soul"—only to wind up severely disappointed. In this case, you've projected your own inner Beloved onto someone in your outer life. And, quite naturally, no one can ever live up to that perfection that you seek. Why this happens is no mystery. Until the hidden material in our psyches is brought to consciousness, we get tricked into acting out an unconscious love life, and often by making the same flawed choice again and again. Projection and unconsciousness go hand in hand.

All romantic relationships, I'm sad to say, tend to mix shadowy and spiritual cravings. We long for that unrequited love of the poets' dream—while simultaneously we want the passion of a real earthy, sexy human partner. If we seek spiritual communion at the expense of our human desires, we risk becoming filled with illusory expectations that are impossible to meet. Conversely, if we ignore our spiritual needs and focus only on our earthly passions, we risk playing out some shadowy Don Juan or femme fatale who lures their prey into seductive fantasies that threaten the balanced life we desire.

Once you bring to consciousness and integrate your projections, your love life moves out of the shadows. You'll discover that your deepest love affair is always with the inner Beloved, your soul. No matter who your earthly partner is, the key to success in any relationship is the inner marriage of your human and divine Self.

What the Shadow Brings to Light

The human shadow's sacred function is to bring to light everything we wish to hide and deny about ourselves, especially our unexamined illusions about love. When we choose to integrate our dark side, we gain stability and an expansion of consciousness, and become flexible instead of rigidly defended. As you bring more of yourself to consciousness, your passion for life is enhanced and you just naturally begin to feel more authentic and alive.

Owning our own shadow is the basis for forgiveness and compassion, which is another of its sacred functions. Since every human being casts a shadow, recognizing our own heals our one-sided self-righteousness and opens our hearts to a loving appreciation of our common humanity. We can all empathize with the politician whose speeches about "upholding the public trust" are scoffed at by revelations of his financial impropriety, or the fire-and-brimstone preacher who is arrested in a vice raid. The shadow is nothing if not democratic, and some time or another, we will all be caught with our dark side exposed.

The Shadow Is All Your Disowned Parts

Paradoxically, your shadow is not all negative traits. It's all your unconscious, unlived potential as well—some still unexpressed talents and gifts you can easily love, once you learn to express them: your lover self, your playful self, your wise woman or wise man self, the leader or artist in you. Any of these can be buried in your shadow. But when unlived, we can become "shadowy" and react with intense criticism born of jealousy when we see someone else expressing our unacknowledged talent. Or, we can project our own denied gift onto another and idolize the person—say, an artist, rather than developing our own latent artistic gift. Or, we might develop strong adoration for a leader who incites our own unacknowledged drive for power.

Do you see how this works? These unexpressed aspects of yourself are energetic and always find a way to make themselves known. The key is staying conscious. Consciousness disempowers the shadow who can only act out when we are "in the dark." The shadow has to be seen in the clear light of day to heal. When exposed, we can "zap it" with our compassion and understanding.

Sometimes revealing the shadow so it can heal requires an act of supreme courage. I remember a powerful example of this that occurred in one of our healing workshops. Participants were asked to dress up in costumes that represented an aspect of their shadow they were ready to heal, and come to group one evening for a "shadow dance." One beautiful, young woman with a history of acting out sexually when she was drunk showed up in a G-string and very little else. At first, we were all shocked. Some of my male staff members felt they needed to leave, and wives were grabbing their husbands in possessive, fearful ways. All of our shadowy feelings about sex, jealousy and possessiveness were activated.

Then, the music came on, and this woman began walking around the room, looking each of us deeply in the eyes. Thankfully, we all fell into our hearts. We honored this revealed aspect of her, bowed to it, and gave her nothing to feel shame about. This process of acknowledgment went on for several minutes. I feel tears coming to my eyes as I recall the woman's brave self-disclosure in our process group the next morning. She wept in gratitude, saying that our acceptance had healed this wounded part of her that had nearly ruined her life.

Owning Your Shadow

Facing the shadow is an essential step along any spiritual journey. You'll find that everyone, even spiritual teachers, are engaged in some kind of personal "shadow dance" at some point in their lives. People who tell you they have no shadow are standing in it as they speak! Failure to do our shadow work is a dangerous avoidance of our human process that leads us into a cul-de-sac of unconscious behavior and blocks our growth.

Just as a masterful potter works with clay, we can learn to shape our personality's behavior with an inner image of our true form. As an aspect of our greater Self, the human shadow creates the "fire by friction" that exposes to the light of consciousness whatever needs to be pared away. So, have compassion for your shadow, who is crying out to be accepted. When you realize that the shadow is that sacred part of you who has the toughest assignment of reminding you of what you've not yet integrated, your heart will open to this unloved part of yourself.

When we try to deny the shadow it multiplies. When we choose to integrate it instead, we gain stability and expansion of consciousness and become flexible instead of rigidly defended. Owning our own shadow makes us more compassionate toward others when they are caught in their shadows. When we can stand on someone's blind side without judgment, we are aiding that person. To be a truly caring person, we can learn to be as at home in the shadow's domain as in the light—well-acquainted with the wilderness experience we, as humans, must all travel through if we are to grow to our full potential.

Remember, whatever is unconscious has power over you. But whatever you make conscious, you can use to help make you whole. The greater Self within you can always rule over these wounded, fragmented selves when we're willing to make them conscious.

THE LIFE LESSON
Embracing Your Shadow

If you feel split between loving and hating parts of yourself and others, shadow work may be the lesson that is up for you right now. Ask yourself: Do I put myself or others down when they behave in ways I don't approve? Am I afraid of revealing my true feelings in some situation? Am I arrogant? Impatient? Always trying to be too "perfect"? Do I gossip or get a secret thrill out of seeing others fail? Do I let emotional reactions run rampant over my life, then say I have no power over them? What kinds of people cause me to overreact in negative or positive ways?

Also explore how your shadow may be impacting your love life. Are you perpetually dissatisfied with your partner, while you nurse a secret fantasy that somewhere out there is your "soul mate" or "twin flame"? Or, do your relationships all seem to fail in the same way for similar reasons?

Regardless of ways your shadow is manifesting, the first step in dealing with it is to lighten up and be a little kinder to yourself. This in itself helps to integrate the shadow. If you catch yourself overreacting to a person or situation, here are clues that you may be projecting an unacknowledged piece of you onto someone else:

• You perceive someone as an "enemy" and yourself as a "victim."

- You perceive someone as a "savior" or as a paragon of virtue and believe that this person holds the key to your salvation.
- You become obsessed with someone else's problems and set about to "do" this person's life.
- You fall madly in love with someone who is not available or appropriate and fantasize about this relationship as the ideal.
- You sacrifice your money, time and energy to some cause that you decide is more important than your own life.

Do any of these sound familiar? If so, you probably have shadow work to do! The following practice this month will help:

THE PRACTICE
Transforming Reactivity

- Bring to consciousness what is causing your reaction and claim the issue as your own.
- Discharge the pent-up feelings appropriately by talking to a reliable therapist or a well-balanced friend. Or, express your feelings privately through tears, an angry journal entry, or a vigorous workout at the gym.
- Transform the energy that remains into some positive expression. Throw yourself into your work, write a poem, draw, paint or garden madly.

The following guided imagery exercise will help you identify some part of your shadow that's ready now to integrate.

Shadow Work
A Guided Imagery

Close your eyes, and envision yourself sitting in an empty room, dressed as you are today. As you sit there, you are reflecting on what part of your shadow may be ready now to come into your conscious mind and heal. As you are thinking about this, you hear a noise coming from underneath the floor in the corner of the room. You realize this is where your shadow is hiding.

Get up now, and walk toward the corner.... Notice there's a trap door there, inviting you to open it and walk in.... You see a violet cloak hanging on a hook and a lit candle sitting on a shelf, so you put on the cloak and take the candle and open the trap door.... Notice how you feel as you walk down the steps....

As the light begins to enter the dark space below, you suddenly see a movement of someone trying to hide from you.... Invite it out.... And see what appears....

Notice how it's dressed.... And what age it is.... Watch it move around and notice how it carries itself.... Which of your qualities does this image hold for you? ...

Now, begin a dialogue with this shadow self. Ask it how long it's been with you.... Let it tell you what it's protecting, and how it came to be....

Merge with this part of yourself and be this shadow self for a moment or two.... Are painful feelings coming up? If so, go into the essence of the pain and discover its root.... Perhaps some old childhood wound.... Maybe someone or a part of yourself you still need to forgive.... Whatever feelings arise, let them "bleed on out".... Do not repress them.... This expression is part of your healing.

Now, with an open heart, tell your shadow that you accept it and watch what happens inwardly.... Tell your shadow that you are inviting it to walk along beside you in life, remembering, of course, that you are the one in charge.... And love it as much as you can from wherever you're at in your visualization.

Then watch what happens in your mind's eye. Take as long as you need for this part of the process. . . . Once you feel some integration taking place, allow these inner images to become a light gray mist.

Take off the cloak, blow out the candle, and walk back to your chair and sit once more, in reflection of all that just occurred in your inner life. . . .

Finally, take some time to process this experience. It's wise to write about or draw an image of your shadow to help integrate it.

CHAPTER TEN

THE FIFTH SELF PRINCIPLE
"Victimhood is a case of mistaken identity"

At this time in history we are to take
nothing personally. Least of all ourselves.
For the moment we do, our spiritual journey
comes to a halt. Banish the word "struggle"
from your attitude and your vocabulary,
and learn to celebrate life.

—The Elders, Hopi Nation

Victimhood is a shadowy, insidious state of consciousness that halts our spiritual journey. Victim consciousness is spawned from a grave misunderstanding about who you are and will cause you to always see life as a struggle you are powerless to overcome. The true Self is an empowered self, never anyone's victim or pawn. It never occurs to the empowered Self to blame anyone else for anything!

There's no denying there is serious abuse in our world—physical, emotional and mental. Though it's an extremely hard reality to have to undergo any kind of harsh abuse, the spiritual wisdom of the world teaches us that everything we experience here serves a sacred purpose for our life and for humanity as a whole. All are lessons in love. Even our birth into a particular family where harmful abuse occurred is part of the sacred design for the human soul's purification and transformation. No event in our life is ever "just personal." In a philosophy of wholeness, your job description as a spiritual being in human form is to come here and take on the human condition and transform it. This is how we bring heaven to earth.

This statement may make you angry or bring up a sense of divine betrayal. "Why," you might be thinking, "do innocent children have to go through sexual abuse? Where is the sacred justice in that?" You're forgetting that babies and small children are big souls in little bodies, and that the strongest, most mature souls are often the ones who take on the hardest lessons.

Understanding Karma

Questions about why we suffer are among life's most difficult mysteries. They have plagued seekers of spiritual truth the world over. Most spiritual paths agree, however, that there is a reason, though we may never know it, why each soul carries the cross that it bears. If we could know all the mysteries of karma and other cosmic laws, such as life's purpose created by the law of attraction, we'd fully understand that our soul knows what it's doing and enters into the lifestream it's most cut out to follow. Among the most transformative lessons we learn as we grow toward spiritual maturity is that there are no victims, even in what appear to be the most heinous atrocities of life.

Such knowledge removes any feeling of being tossed about by the hands of fate, or by evil people. It brings us face-to-face with our sacred cocreative responsibilities here as daughters and sons of God. The "victim/perpetrator" syndrome is a state of consciousness, both sides happening on the same level, swinging back and forth. Cops create robbers; robbers create cops. To overcome this archetypal plight, you must rise above it, like the top point of a triangle, to a third and higher station in consciousness—one where you can take full responsibility for your life.

The purpose of this Life Principle is to help awaken you to this realization.

Victim consciousness is based on our ignorance of three fundamental truths:

- All our suffering has a sacred purpose.
- Though we cannot avoid suffering, we do have the power to control how we respond to life's misfortunes.
- All lessons in life are lessons in love.

The Sacred Purpose of Human Suffering

The sacred purpose of suffering is to help us transform and grow into our Self and live in a state of bliss. For instance, when a betrayal or relationship failure plummets you into victimhood, if you're willing to be conscious, you can look back and see how you sowed the seeds of your own betrayal. Perhaps you idolized the person in a way no one could ever live up to. Or you innocently ignored warnings about how this betrayal was destined to occur.

I remember a particularly poignant demonstration in one of our workshops of how we set up victim consciousness. A man had made it plain to us that he was the "wounded child." When it came time to do a process requiring a partner, he demanded to work with someone who would not "abandon" him. He went on and on about this. The woman who volunteered for the role was a very caring person who vowed she would "be there" for him. The man felt relieved and lay down to do the two-hour music meditation with closed eyes, while his partner served as his protector. During the whole lengthy process, this woman stood watch over his space with a deep sense of commitment. Right toward the end, she scooted away for about twenty seconds to put a blanket over a neighboring participant. At just that moment, the man sat straight up, opened his eyes, and yelled, "See! I told you this would happen!" Later, he made a major breakthrough about his part in this lifelong process.

Struggle will always be a natural part of any creation. There is a natural law of creativity, always made up of three components for anything to be made: *thesis, antithesis* and *synthesis*. The *thesis* is the issue or the desired experience—anything new that we are learning. The *antithesis* process is the culling out of all that distorts or ruins the thesis, such as unlove. This is where pain and difficulties will naturally be experienced. It's the trial and error part of any new creation. The synthesis is the final, purified result, once our practice has taught us what works and what does not.

For example, you may be learning how to be a good parent for your first child—or a good business partner in your first business venture. You've gained your ideas about what a "good parent" or "a successful business partner" are from others and from society at large. Or perhaps you've studied a lot of books from the experts on these matters. Then, your child is born, or your business is incorporated. And you are thrown into the living experience of being good at these new experiences. Perhaps there is some illusion in what you've learned. Or perhaps your child or new partner just doesn't conform to the ideal, so that your beliefs about good parenting or good business are tested to the hilt. You struggle. You suffer.

As you consciously practice any new endeavor in life, you learn what works as an effective, wise and considerate way to be, and what does not. You go through the fire in making mistakes, or by listening to advice from others that turns out to be useless or even harmful. Sometimes, during the antithesis stage, there are harsh lessons to endure. You may feel you've failed or been betrayed by another. Finally, though, if you pursue, you wind up naturally good at what you set out to learn in your own way, through having remained conscious and taken responsibility for your own trial and error experience.

Reflect on this, and you'll see that falling into victimhood or low self-esteem over the *antithesis* part of anything in life is simply a misunderstanding of how life works. Blaming others or falling into shame for our mistakes is a nongrowth choice. As whole people, we will grow into gratitude for this cosmic process of Creativity and honor the antithesis part for its sacred purpose. Experiencing what doesn't work in any new venture in life weeds out the antithetical parts and leads us to transcendence. Some of our greatest teachers turn out to be those who have been our adversaries, or taking on challenging projects where there was a lot to learn.

Victim, Scapegoat, Enemy, Orphan, Betrayer—all these self-created roles bring us archetypal "labors of love" to help awaken us to our true nature. When we overcome our victim consciousness, we begin to deepen our commitment to live our life to the fullest and reconnect with our true purpose for being here.

Compassion and Forgiveness Heal Suffering

Though we cannot avoid suffering, we can learn to respond to it with compassion for those who have caused us to suffer and for ourselves for having undergone the misery. Forgiving those who have harmed us is one of the most healing aspects of divine Love. When we forgive someone, we naturally relinquish some pattern of self-righteousness or one-sided thinking. Our greater Self knows that letting go of blame, including self-blame, is essential to our well-being.

I had an alcoholic mother who, after years of inner work, I've been able to forgive. She was a naturally loving and warm person, who allowed alcoholism to turn her into the opposite of who she wanted to be. As I matured, I felt deep sorrow for all her unrealized potential and for how she had so disappointed herself. My mother taught me compassion for the sick and wounded and pointed me to my true life's work. She may have even sacrificed her own happiness to teach me this. Who knows? We just never know the truth of someone else's karma or sacred purpose. Who are we, ever, to judge?

As a therapist, I have seen there are people who've unknowingly made victimhood their profession, using guilt to coerce others into doing what they want. It's like the old joke about the adult son who telephones his elderly mother.

"How are you, Mother?" the son asks.

"Not so good," the mother replies.

"What's wrong?" the son asks with concern.

"I haven't eaten in seventeen days."

"Seventeen days!" the son replies. "Why not? What's wrong?"

"I didn't want my mouth to be full when you finally called."

If you have a perpetual victim in your family, it's hard not to fall into the trap of thinking that it's your responsibility to "save" this person. This is not love; it's codependence, and it holds the pattern of victimhood firmly in place.

Every victim needs a perpetrator. Victim consciousness keeps you focused on the "enemy out there," on someone who "owes you something." This view disempowers you and sets up the conditions for you to suffer again and again. As long as you expect yourself to be a victim, a string of "perpetrators" will stretch far into your future life, as far as you can imagine. Ironically, it's your thinking that creates the concept "perpetrator"! And even more ironically, victims can turn into perpetrators when they go after "those out there who have done them harm." The victim-perpetrator process works like a pendulum, swinging from one role to the other. Whatever you obsess about and feed emotion into will manifest. You really are this powerful.

You can build whatever reality you want, not by changing your outer circumstances or anything that's already been set in motion, but by carefully constructing the mental image of where you'd like to go from here and who you'd like to be. If you honor your past for the good it's given you, you can stop wasting your precious energy by looking back in a victim-perpetrator stance. You can step confidently into the divine plan for humanity's future, and start focusing on your part in its unfolding.

THE LIFE LESSON
Being Seated in Your Own Power

If you are identified as being the victim of life in general, or of anyone in particular, you are in grave spiritual trouble. You are giving your power away to something or someone, forgetting who you really are. Perpetrators will surround you, real or imagined. You'll know if this life lesson applies to you.

In most cases, we can get to the bottom of how we help co-create our feelings of "victim." If your suffering is manifesting as a lack of financial resources, you can ask yourself how generous you have been to others—and to yourself. Perhaps you simply took on a primary relative's attitude toward money and never developed an attitude of your own. Or, you may be addicted to the feeling of not being worthy of abundance. If you are suffering from loneliness or feelings of being left out, ask yourself whether you can really be a good companion to yourself, or to others. Do you unconsciously set up your life so you are alone? Do you deliberately choose isolation?

If your suffering has manifested as physical illness, examine whether your condition has come about to teach you to reevaluate what's important in life. Or, perhaps you are to heal your disease by using the natural laws of healing and a reidentification with that greater one in you who is never sick. Maybe you are to model this for the rest of us. Surely you do know that some have overcome even the worst cases of cancer or muscular dystrophy.

The universe says "yes" to whatever we call our truth and turns it into our reality. No one can escape the cosmic law of cause and effect. To overcome feelings of victimhood, you can learn to rule your life with a scepter and not a sword. Now, what on earth do I mean when I say that? Symbolically, a sword cuts things in two: "It's me against you." Whereas a scepter symbolizes the quiet rule of the centered Self who is seated in its power: "You and I are one." The empowered Self holds a scepter, not a sword, for it knows that everything is connected and nothing has to be fought, just honored and recognized for what it truly is, then treated as such in right relationship.

A scepter, or a wand, symbolizes the spiritual or creative dimension of consciousness. Wave a magic wand, and you can change the picture of something in a flash. Unlike the warrior who rules with a sword, the spiritual warrior wins over opposition through love and creativity. Our world is starving for this gentler ruling style of the spiritual warrior.

If you generally wield a sword, you may wish to ask yourself whether this harshness is doing more harm than good. If you feel you lack the will or the ability to make positive changes in your life, you may have become your own oppressor. The sword of self-denial is keeping you down more effectively than any external enemy or circumstance.

Even if you've made some horrible mistake or have taken a wrong turn, see if you can be gentle with yourself while owning "your part" in the predicament. Try to recognize some new talent or positive quality you've been incubating that you haven't yet noticed you possess. This new quality or talent may be the very one you're being asked to birth now to overcome any tendency toward victimhood.

The following exercise may help you step beyond victim consciousness on your expedition to reclaim your whole Self.

THE PRACTICE
Observing Victimhood

Remember, the Victim is a subpersonality. It's one that we all have to a certain degree. It overtakes our conscious Self anytime we feel slighted, betrayed, abused, neglected or taken advantage of. During this month, use your Observer Self to notice if and when you feel any of these negative feelings toward your life situations or the people with whom you relate.

In your "little book," write down any time one of these feelings comes over you. And note the story line you are using to feel victimized. Then, take some time to own your part in whatever is happening that's causing you to have these feelings. Be radically honest with yourself!

As you observe the various times you feel like a victim of something or someone, ask yourself what positive quality you would need to overcome this feeling. Courage? Discrimination? Acceptance of what is? Then, invoke this positive quality and practice taking it on. With your imagination, you can create a positive subpersonality to overcome any debilitating or weak side that feels victimized. How about a Viking King? Or a Goddess on a White Steed? Be willing to become that which is missing in you to transcend any evidence of victimhood in your life. Victimhood breeds powerlessness. You no longer need this, so let it go.

The following imagery will help bring you back to your Self.

Reclaiming Your Freedom
A Guided Imagery

When you are trapped in victim consciousness, you feel yourself to be at the mercy of someone or something. "What's the use of fighting it?" you say. "I can't win in this situation. Or if I do, something will come along and ruin it anyway."

If this is your pattern, take some time now to close your eyes and go into a reflective state.... Get in touch fully with this feeling.

Go back in time now, and remember a situation in which you allowed yourself to feel victimized and how uncomfortable it was to lose your sense of control or feel so powerless....

If guilt arises about having caused yourself to suffer in this way, remember that laying a guilt trip on yourself is just another form of victimhood. So allow the guilt to pass on by and do not attach to it. . . . Instead, let yourself get more lighthearted about how you sometimes play victim, and see this self in you plainly. . . . Now, give it a humorous name, like "Pitiful Polly" or "Wilting Willie."

And with all your heart, let a sense of compassion and warmth flow over you for this wounded little fragment of your ego. . . . Let it speak to you now and tell you of its woes. . . . Let it feel heard. . . . Tell it you forgive it for the limitations it has caused you, that you understand it was only trying to help. . . . And now, release this sub-personality with love. . . . As its image dissipates, feel its essence coming into your heart as its positive side, which is *caution* and careful *discrimination* concerning who to give your heart or precious energy to. . . . As you do this, note the you who is embracing this part of yourself, for this powerful one is who you truly are. . . .

Take some time to feel anchored in your real Self. . . . Watch how you stand, note how you behave. . . . And imagine making a decision to act from now on in this freedom to be your Self.

CHAPTER ELEVEN

THE SIXTH SELF PRINCIPLE

"Your desire nature is God's love living in you"

If one follows what I call one's "bliss"—
the thing that really gets you deep
in the gut and that you feel is your life—
doors will open.

—Joseph Campbell

What Is Desire Anyway?

Desires are the hopes and wishes your dreams are made of—the fuel that drives your interests. Your desires are your longings, your attractions and your passions. This is one of the hardest psychospiritual truths for us to assimilate because of our religious imprinting. We've often been warned to fear human desires and to repress them as shameful or less than spiritual. Or, we're told to never allow strong feelings to show. And it's certainly true that strong feelings can be chaotic and overwhelming, and when captured by a desire, we can feel out of control. So we block them.

Strong attractions do indeed come upon us like Fate; they manifest beyond our intellect's control. For instance, what is it, do you suppose, that attracts you so strongly to another human being? It's certainly not the intellect. You know that it's impossible to make yourself feel in love with someone, no matter how logical or perfect that choice might seem. Therefore, we must conclude that every magnetic pull we feel comes from a deeper place within us and contains either a necessary lesson or a soul expression seeking to come forth. Our desires are our motivating force, the cosmic Law of Attraction in operation in our lives.

Some spiritual paths even tell us we are to "kill off desire" and starve our human needs for gratification if we are to be spiritual. This, however, is a violation of psychological law, the law of human nature. The saddest, most frustrated people I know are those who hold themselves away from living, afraid they are violating spiritual law by allowing themselves to enjoy being human.

When a strong human desire is squelched, this becomes an unmet need that gets buried in the closet of repression and denial in your subconscious mind, and then, this need will act out when you least expect it. The married minister gets caught in the arms of a lover. The perfect couple wind up in a devastating custody battle.

One of the most important tasks on the sacred journey to wholeness is learning to trust that your desires are how God's love translates into a human heart. Everything you're drawn to is a reminder of something you need to feel whole, even though what you might need may be a tough lesson. Otherwise you wouldn't feel the pull so acutely; there would be no interest.

If you'll think back over your personal love story, you'll see that every attraction contained a necessary soul expression or lesson about love and unlove that needed to be made known. You can trust that the true desires of your heart—what mythologist Joseph Campbell calls "our bliss"—are compelling nudges that come straight from the Self.

The key is to know yourself well enough that you can discriminate between a soul desire and a compulsive ego need. A desire coming from your soul feels like an intense yearning to be someone greater—someone more spiritual, more loving, or further along in your life's work and expression of your true Self. You can actually feel this desire as a yearning in your heart. This is a fourth level of consciousness desire that comes from love. A soul desire will always lead you to a better place and never causes harm to yourself or another.

An ego desire, on the other hand, is felt as a pressure in your gut, like a clutched feeling in your stomach. This is a third level of consciousness urge toward some unfinished psychological business, which may need to be recognized, acknowledged for its desire, and then contained. The compulsive and addictive cravings of a needy ego can give you valuable information about your unmet needs— that is, *if you remain conscious.* You can learn to discipline the ways you allow these ego needs to act out. Once you know what the desire is, you can often find a healthy way to meet the real need buried under what might be masquerading as an ego drive for power or attention. Do you see what I mean? You learn to ask yourself, "What's *really* going on here? What am I really seeking?"

People with serious addiction problems know that place of urgency that says "I want what I want when I want it," with little thought of consequences. Sugar binges, sexual acting out, getting drunk, or wasted on drugs, and sometimes even violent outbursts of emotion can be the disastrous result. Acting out base desires has extreme consequences such as prison terms, the loss of prestige or success, the loss of family and friends, and public humiliation. We all know this. Yet, any one of these may be prices necessary for an obstinate personality to pay to get the lesson, or to learn that one's addiction needs treatment. An "old timer" in AA once warned me: "Don't you ever take pain away from a drunk! It's what will eventually lead him to health."

The intensity of your desire nature is what will eventually lead you to the fulfillment of your ideals. Therefore, we never want to denigrate what we long for or seek to destroy our passions through mechanisms of repression. Denying our true feelings is a seedbed for shadow and a contaminated, pseudo spirituality. Whether a desire is straight from your soul or from an unmet ego need, discounting or repressing the urge to express it is never appropriate psychologically. Repression activates the shadow, and you can bet it will act out your unacknowledged desire in unconscious ways you'll feel awful about later. I'm sure you can relate. How often have you been embarrassingly caught in a jealous temper fit, or flirting with someone's mate, or gossiping about a good friend—only to realize later it was all about you.

Emotionalism Reshapes
Your Biochemical/Neural Network

The science behind mind-body medicine has found that our emotions are constantly regulating what we experience as "reality." The decision about what sensory information travels in your brain and what gets filtered out depends on what signals the receptors are receiving from the neuropeptides released by brain cells. According to Dr. Candace Pert:

"Peptides are the sheet music containing the notes, phrases, and rhythms that allow the orchestra—your body—to play as an integrated entity. And the music that results is the tone or feeling that you experience subjectively as your emotions."[10]

The brain, as the source of our emotional states, carries this emotional information to our tissues, organs, heart, blood vessels, stomach, and even to our immune system. Consequently, our emotions reshape our receptor cells and become addictive from being acted out over and over. Our emotional responses, these researchers believe, are guiding our choices in life. By consistently practicing new and healthy ways of responding emotionally, we can heal our emotions and carve new neural pathways into our cellular structure.[11]

As true seekers on a spiritual path to wellness, we learn the right use of our feeling powers, to not fear our passions, nor to ever misuse them. Those of you who can feel passion strongly are the "muses of the soul." You never want your light to burn dim; it's not your nature to be dull or uncreative. Your heart's desires are how God's Love pours into your life and guides you along your unique way of expression and fulfillment.

It's Symptom or Symbol, Which Do You Prefer?

We purify our desire nature, our emotional body, through "acting out" or through "acting in." The more you can "act in," the less you'll need to "act out." Acting out is the ego's way of healing you. It's the way of projection. You have a symbolic need to be right vis-à-vis a male authority figure, so you have a bitter fight with your professor that gets you thrown out of school.

"Acting in" is the soul's way of healing you. Through inner work, you go through the images and subjective awarenesses and feelings this problem represents and heal the issue from the inside out.

Committing to the path of inner work saves you from problems that arise when you project your unmet needs onto others. When we're unable to acknowledge or express an unfulfilled inner need, we often blame other people or life in general for denying us what we desire.

THE LIFE LESSON
Healing Your Emotional Body

You can see now how crucial it is to your well-being that your emotional body heal. Apparently, our emotions are not only creating disease in our mental attitudes, they are reshaping our biochemical structure as well!

So for now, let's presume that your passions are leading you to the lessons you need in learning to express true love in life. And we all need these lessons. Accepting this as your task will remove shame and blame concerning whatever you may be craving "high" or "low."

You realize you must take responsibility for your emotional reactions and are never to act on any desires that would cause harm to yourself or to anyone else. So here's what you do when a strong desire or craving strikes:

- Go ahead and *feel* the desire (which you won't be able to help feeling anyway, so really go into it) and then be honest about what it is you are truly longing for.

- Imagine yourself acting out this desire, and take it all the way through to the end of the story, consequences or end results.

- Now, in your mind, contemplate the urge that caused you to act out; think it through to determine whether it's a true heart desire or an egoistic compulsion that cannot lead to good. Where do you feel it in your body?

- Write in your "little book" all you need to about desiring this particular thing. Write furiously, until all the energy has drained off of the subject. Then see what is the underlying desire that's driving the passion. What do you feel you lack?

If it's an ego need, it will be coming from one of the lower chakras—a need to feel safe and protected, a need for intimacy and belonging, a need for self-confidence or higher self-esteem. Bottom line: the lower chakra needs are needs to be noticed and loved or appreciated for who you are.

Through this kind of radical self-honesty, you can then find a way to meet the desire in a conscious, healthy fashion.

THE PRACTICE
Learning to Stand "at Nil"

A Guided Imagery

If you feel you often have imbalanced or extreme emotional overreactions, often at the mercy of your feeling nature, you will benefit from learning to stand at the nil point in your psyche. It will keep you in your center, at the zero point, safely balanced between the two sides of any emotional extremism.

Find a quiet place where you can be alone for a while. Let your body relax and your mind settle down.

Close your eyes and envision that you are standing in the center of a circle. You are the point in the middle, standing tall in all your potency as a soul in human form. . . . Anchor this feeling by envisioning it clearly and intensely for a moment. . . .

Now imagine an invisible line of force making a circle going over your head and under your feet, from the back to the front of you. . . . Imagine a second line encircling your body now (like a hula hoop would do). . . . So that now you are completely encircled over, under, and all around. Feel the enclosure as a safe container, holding you away from any outside influences. . . . And know that you are inside this container like a bubble, where nothing from behind you, before you, or from either side can influence your emotions. . . .

Feel the bubble becoming "pregnant" with warmth and complete silence. . . . Perfect peace. . . .

Take awhile to anchor this feeling, then come back into your ordinary reality, knowing that you can throw up this "bubble" like opening an umbrella, in the twinkling of an eye, anytime you start to feel overpowered by an unwanted emotion, or someone else's unwanted energy.

Invoking Love and Inspiration
A Guided Imagery

You may be someone who, instead of feeling too much chaotic emotion, rarely feels much at all. You lack passion in your life and often feel there's nothing to get interested in or thrilled about.

Eros is the beautiful god of love and inspiration who rekindles the spiritual fires of our passion for living. He is a living spirit in your psyche. He makes possible a constant revival of soul. When we feel ourselves to be in love—with some activity, some person, or just with life itself—we are vibrant with life force and connected to Spirit.

You can access Eros through your creative imagination anytime you are feeling this listlessness, or an inability to love.

Close your eyes and see what Eros looks like as you image him in your mind. . . . Let the energies of this inner Beloved penetrate your heart and fill your entire body with feelings of warmth and love. . . .

Now, think of someone you love or have loved—a person or an animal. . . . Allow your imagination to play over every feeling, every memory, every physical sensation connected with this love. Really let yourself experience this. . . .

Now, allow these feelings of love to carry you to some project, artistic creation, or work you are currently undertaking, and feel the love and inspiration as a warm rush coursing through your mind and heart. . . . And bless this project with love.

Allow Eros to be revealed to you once more, and hear the message he is whispering in your ear. . . . Thank him for what he's given you, and feel yourself slowly returning to your ordinary reality.

Take some time to reflect on any message you may have received, and write about it in your journal. And know that communing with Eros is available to you any time you feel a lack of spirit in your life. Know that you have found an inner partner and the joy of a secret love who will remain with you forever.

CHAPTER TWELVE

THE SEVENTH SELF PRINCIPLE

"We learn to live within the tension of opposites as 'walkers in two worlds'"

All God-things come in pairs.

—Carl Jung

Dualism Is a Reality on the Physical Plane

Can you think of any quality of life that does not have its exact opposite? I am certain that you can't, because everything in life has its flip side. Love, unlove; right, wrong; success, failure; conscious, unconscious ... and on we go. The nature of this material reality is dual, and there's a sacred purpose for this. We learn how to love by experiencing unlove. We feel successful because we know failure. We know when we're on track in our lives by experiencing what it feels like to be offtrack. To actually know true union, we must first experience the illusion of separateness. We "fell" from the uncreated spiritual world into this created world of matter—and thereby experienced our first duality: we came from the *uncreated* into the *created*.

The Self is a whole battery of opposites precisely because there can be no reality without polarity. Light does not exist until it strikes an object. Both sides of any opposition compose a sacred truth. In fact, you could say one side could not even exist without the other. If the One let go of the Other, it would lose its character. And, these two push themselves away from each other to exist at all. Thus there arises a tension of opposites. Standing in the tension of opposites requires that you understand and accept that the Divine has two faces and that, to be whole, the Self honors both.

Uniting the Opposites

All opposites within us are "lovers" seeking to unite. In true Love there is no carpet under which anything can be swept. All is seen, felt and acknowledged as having value. This is true accountability. The psychic function of any split we ever feel happening within us is to create the "fire by friction" that keeps forcing us to resolve it. We swing back and forth on a pendulum of personal angst until some higher level is reached, where the issue can "come clear" in a whole newly created way of knowing it.

To ever transcend a contradictory situation in life, we must first experience its two sides separately, the light and the shadow, the "yes" and the "no" of it. Opposites are equally impactful. We can drop judgment of either side by understanding that duality is creativity in motion. Then we can learn to make each opposition within us complementary rather than conflictual. When too much energy is poured into either/or thinking, we lose our balance. And balance, or living "the middle way," will always be the higher way.

So this is our work. When something integrates, we can see the sacred in all our contradictions and the creative "friction" they provide.

The Nature of Duality

In duality, you either hate them or love them. In unity, you accept them for who and what they are. In duality, you are either a success or a failure. In transcendence, you are just exactly where you are, with no judgment. Nothing is in denial; nothing is left out. Through experiencing the tension of the opposites, all is brought to authentic wholeness on a third and higher level of consciousness. If we allow ourselves to only experience the positive side of any pole, we will have complete naiveté about how its shadow operates. Then, we'll be knocked off our feet at some point by our ignorance. Until we recognize and honor this principle of life, we will bounce back and forth in either/or living, or we'll be lopsided, trying with utter futility to live from only the positive side of the pole, or else trapped and hopeless in the negative side. Wisdom comes from having experienced it all. From either/or to both/and leads to wisdom. Finding that "third and higher thing" is the Law of Transcendence in full force.

So, anytime you have a conflictual pair of opposites driving you to drink, tell yourself you are going to transcend the split. Then, as you willingly get to know and accept both sides of your dilemma, you'll see how when "rubbed together" each pair creates a third and higher quality. For example, when your laziness jostles your driving overachiever, a balanced efficiency is born. When your tightfisted side jostles your flamboyant big spender, you can thoroughly enjoy the pleasure of making "good buys."

You hear people say we are to live in unity consciousness, that there is no such thing as duality. This is a misunderstanding. The highest truth is, of course, *all is one*. Yet, life on a creation planet such as Earth is an *antinomy—two total opposites living harmoniously together making up one whole*. The symbol best representing this apparent duality is the Chinese Yin/Yang—a circle containing a curving dark side with a point of light in it, and a curving light side with a point of dark in it, living together as one. Some call this the marriage of the masculine and feminine principles, who are capable of creating reality.

When the Self, as our consciousness, enters any apparent duality, it actually functions as a triad, which, at the highest point of any two conflicting opposites, becomes the integration point. In human bodies, we perceive separation before we transcend it— and so, at the two lower arms of the triangle, we battle with the opposites. This "fire by friction" is how creativity, or "the law of three," operates. It's how we arrive at that third and higher way of doing or being anything. Einstein told us we can never solve a problem on the same level upon which it was created.

"The light, the dark, no difference," instructs physician and spiritual teacher Brugh Joy. The Self knows how to include the wisdom from both sides of the polarity—the dark and the light, the human and the divine—by "knowing" each other's nature. The shadow has shadow nature; the light functions as light. It therefore can integrate and transcend the two into the oneness from whence it originated.

The Transcendent Function

Trying to live just at the top misses the point of creation: the process of struggling with the opposites, known in Jungian therapy as "the transcendent function," takes you beyond the tension. We rest at the zero point in the middle, yet on a higher plane of understanding. We cannot deny the process of the warring opposites, without landing in an ungrounded reality. To realize unity requires our acceptance and integration of *both sides* of the polarities. Otherwise, one side has been left unintegrated and will become shadow and act out unconsciously. If you ponder this for a moment, you will see how logical this is. How could we ever be whole if we are only dealing with one side of anything while denying or negating the other side?

To progress on the spiritual journey, you must face the divine ordeal of knowing just how to relate to all of yourself, and to all of human life, both the shadow *and* the light, which often gets polarized into both the human and the spiritual. When seen in their true nature, both sides have a sacred function. Perhaps you have felt this opposition within yourself and not understood its sacred and eternal nature. You could be in peril of being swept away by the dark side of life, addicted to your misery, or terrified by all the suffering here—war, hunger, disease, cruelty, humanity's misery. If you lose your footing, you risk falling into the darkness of depression and loss of meaning. You could stop believing in God, or think life isn't worth living.

Your Task Is Standing "at Nil"

As you face the darkness in this world, you bring consciousness to any activity, standing tall in your true identity as a "light bearer," as one who is willing to meet the dark on its own terms, fearing it not, and matching its strength. Standing firm "at nil," the point at which the magnetic pull of the two contrary poles is equal, feels like living calmly in nonattachment. You are able to think and act clearly, without overreacting to either extreme.

Our commitment to experience the whole thing is the dance of incarnation itself. All addictions and human dysfunction live in the extremes. Self-acceptance, just as you are, resides at the top at the unified point. "The light, the dark, no difference."

Now, let me explain something very important: To own some dark aspect of yourself doesn't mean you have to act it out or give it power over you. It means that you acknowledge the contrary feelings or desires as a part of you and treat them according to their nature. A scorpion has scorpion nature. Your shadow has shadow nature. Your Self has a creative human/divine nature. So you treat each with the respect of *what is*.

Anytime you feel trapped by some apparent opposition, stop and ask yourself, "What is the nature of this whatever I'm needing to understand? What am I really dealing with here?" With your willingness to enter each side of the polarity—just to check it out—the answer will come. The light of consciousness is the transformer.

Opposites Are Lovers Seeking to Unite

How might this necessary complexity of opposites manifest for you in a life-giving fashion? The human side of any conflict will cast a shadow, as it's made of concrete form. So we can call it "the dark." The spiritual side is formless and casts no shadow, so we call it "the light." Let's look now at some examples:

In your work life, your passion (the dark) and your spiritual purpose (the light) can join to become an impassioned vocation. In your relationship life, human sexuality (the dark) and spiritual love (the light) can raise your lovemaking to the level of awesome joy. Appetite (the human side) and delicious food (the spiritual side) can make a meal a feast for the senses and a spiritual offering to the gods. Human anger and grief (the dark) in an opera singer's voice (the light) can turn a song into a celebration of heartfelt triumph over adversity. You must always remember that both aspects of your nature have something precious to give you. When the Divine connects with physical form in balance and harmony, Beauty and Love are made visible.

The opposites within us never forget the One from which they've sprung and to which they long to return: the passionate, spontaneous self and the dry, controlling intellect. Trust and mistrust. The calm and excitable side of human nature. The ego's need to be a material success and the soul's higher calling. These opposites are magnetically attracted to one another like "lovers," yearning to relate. When you recognize these dualities as belonging together, you'll begin to feel more comfortable in your own skin.

You'll feel even more comfortable with the contraries you contain if you remember that every apparently negative quality carries a hidden gift. Look underneath your anger, and you'll find that you've been misusing the energy of enthusiasm. Greed is highlighting your need to fill in some deficiency. If you're jealous of a quality you see in someone else, you probably have the capacity to develop that quality yourself. Look for the transcendent quality in everything, and you'll find the magical sacred buried in the ordinary all around you. Try it. You'll see.

The Self's main task is to aid humanity in dissolving dualism—helping it learn to *live within the tension of the complementary inner opposites.* Every tension of opposites culminates in a release that resolves the tension, out of which comes a new synthesis. Our job here on earth is to hasten this joining. As you practice standing "at nil," accepting and treating naturally both sides of any "twoness," you carve a pathway for the Self to enter and take you to that third and higher way.

THE LIFE LESSON
Closing the Door to Dualism

So what are you to do with these contrary opposites that drive you this way and that—and sometimes plummet you into utter confusion or a paralyzed indecision? The illusion is that you are to try to be positive all the time, and squash the negative pull. Unfortunately, there is a paradox here: the more we ignore the unwanted side, the bigger it grows. The dark side must be met with the nonreactive acknowledgment of what it is—just seeing it and naming it. Trying to be "positive only" will strengthen the negative side and create more shadow; and what's more, you will have a mere surface understanding of the whole issue. The light, the dark, and the transcendent third and higher place provide depth and context to the entire issue at hand.

If you're studying this Principle and feel a response, you are perhaps caught up in one side of a polarity, loving the one while shirking the other. What is it? Get clear, and, in your mind, allow yourself to explore the disowned side. See what you may be in denial of, projecting on someone else, or what it is you need to face. It may be part of your passionate nature you'd be happier to have consciously accessible to you—perhaps some aspect of your sexuality or a deep passion for something. Or you may be enviously noticing a talent in someone else, because that very talent lies unexpressed in *you*.

Through acceptance of both sides of any opposite, the door to dualism closes. This is the lesson that teaches us the paradox of how we truly create the third and higher unity consciousness that contains the wisdom and potency of both sides. And it's never through denying or disowning either side. What good is the light if it cannot find an expression in concrete form? What good is the dark if you do not understand its gift and act it out unconsciously as shadow? You need to see that all opposites are complementary, each requiring the other for its very existence.

Realize that anytime two opposites are rubbing against your psyche in an energetic manner, something is in the very process of transcending. You are "a work in progress." When you can see it this way, you'll find that acceptance of your plight becomes not only possible, but an interesting challenge with a sacred purpose. You then can deal with the issues in life as a courageous spiritual warrior, rather than as one who feels helpless or hopeless.

Questions to Ask Yourself

So ask yourself right now: What kind of duality am I currently caught up in? Is there something in my life that I'm experiencing as "either/or" that needs to unify? Am I making something or someone totally wrong while I'm seeing myself as totally right? Then, watch out. You are headed for a giant disillusionment.

Go within and feel into this current emotional difficulty you are having. Once you can feel it, see the illusion that has trapped you. Look both extremes squarely in the face. Enter into them and feel them for a moment. Learn to know each side from the inside out. When you can see the value in both sides, return to center and integrate what you learned, and watch it transcend into a new and more conscious way of thinking, doing or being.

See if the lesson has anything to do with your dependence on something you are using to make you feel okay, versus learning to be comfortable with who you are. Are you polarizing the inner and the outer, believing the outer is where all your enjoyment and passion lies? Or, conversely, are you living in the mystical world of the inner life, unwilling to take some needed action in the outer

world? Or is there something negative in your current life experience that you just don't want to face, so instead, you are trying to
live as positive only.

Perhaps you've become imbalanced in your inner masculine
and feminine sides. The masculine principle is the one that pulls
us toward assertion and expression with the directness of focused
power and intention. It functions more as the mind. The feminine
principle within each of us is the part that pulls us toward acceptance, and more honoring of all differences, with heartfelt compassion. It functions more as the heart. The masculine acts and
protects; the feminine accepts and caresses. One is not better than
the other; one is not complete without the other. Make note of
your own balance or imbalance of these two sacred principles,
who manifest all creation.

If you are being confronted with something undesirable you do
not wish to deal with, instead of fighting it, try this: Acknowledge
the opposition, even lightheartedly. In your mind's eye, "kiss it on
the cheek" to let it know that it's been seen. Then go about your
business in a conscious, loving manner, taking any necessary action
with heartfelt compassion. Sometimes it's as simple as that.

If this is your lesson, you are being asked now to no longer
battle the opposing factor in yourself or in another by becoming
fanatically one-sided. You need not be at the mercy of the negativity any extremism creates. Your true Self wishes to be reinstated
as the master of its host. Your awakening will accelerate with more
grace as you face the polar opposites within and around you with
ease. No longer are you to be a self divided. The door to dualism is
closing.

It's wonderful to realize that you never have to deny any part of
your human self to be spiritual. You only have to be willing to be
conscious at all times of what's going on inside of you and how

you're expressing it. Remember, you are a spiritual being learning to be human. What's more, you have the capacity to stand tall in your centered Self, whatever contrary winds swirl around you. The exercise that follows will show you how.

THE PRACTICE
Exploring Extremes

All emotional addictions live in the extremes of either/or attitudes and beliefs. Take some time this month to get to know which "causes" in life create emotional tension in you. Explore with deep honesty any extreme reaction you have to anything at all. The extremes can live in your mental body as extreme ideas or fanatical beliefs. In your emotional body, you can feel the extremes as wanting to fight or yell to hold your position about something. In your physical body, extremes manifest as sickness, such as nervous stomach, anxiety or panic attacks, insomnia, and stress-related diseases. Make note of any of these symptoms in your life, and get to the bottom of the emotional addiction and story line reinforcing the symptoms.

Seeing Double
An Ongoing Daily Practice

As hybrid "spirit-matter" beings, we must realize it is appropriate for us to be living in two worlds at once—the world of the human ego and the world of the soul. They are not to become one watered-down nondescript composite. They each bring forth their entire way of being—which is a very rich and inviting way to live: the ego's passionate response to the physical life lives alongside the soul's spiritual purpose and vital intent. In this manner, nothing gets lost. You are learning the art of "seeing double."

You walk the ways of the ordinary life, performing your daily routines with the people who reside in this world with you. You never shirk your responsibilities here. Some are karmic duties, such as caring for children you've birthed or adopted, or helping the elderly in your family life. You do in this world what it is that you've taken on. And you do it with love and compassion. And you help to relieve suffering wherever you go, with all whom you meet along your way.

Together with all this, you hold within you that "secret place" no one, except perhaps a spiritual guide, even needs to know exists for you—unless you have companions with whom you are comfortable sharing your spiritual life. In this inner life—of visions, dreams, symbolic images, inner guides and beings, places in other dimensions you can access, and messages of direct knowing—you document your larger life in your spiritual diary or other form of artwork or creative expression. And you protect this inner "secret place" with all your spiritual might by surrounding it with a deep sense of reverence for your soul.

You walk in the overlap between these worlds, drawing first from one, then from the other. Sometimes you move into just one or the other to give it your full attention. We are always in the process of "breathing in and breathing out." When the in-breath times are upon you, the inner life calls you more; when in an out-breathing stage, your outer life will require your attention. You'll know which is right, and when. Your ego and soul, when aligned, do this work autonomously, without much intellect needed at all.

If you're studying this principle and feel a response, you are being trained in this new way of being. So ask yourself: Have you gotten too mundane and "earthy," perhaps feeling that it's wrong to have your inner life? Or, conversely, have you buried yourself so much in your inner life, you've become "no earthly good"?

This new way of being will always contain the gift from both sides of the equation—with both the passionate human response and the calmness of the one "who knows." Try it. You'll see.

"The Light, the Dark, No Difference"
A Mantra for Living in Balance

Learning to live within the tension of the opposites requires practice living at ease with the attitude of "the light, the dark, no difference." You can actually make this a mantra to say over and over to yourself anytime you feel you're getting hooked in some polarity. Practice just letting things be, not getting caught up in other people's "stuff," and go about your own business of meeting your goals and highest intentions.

As you walk through your days this month, notice how tense you become when you feel you have to "take sides" in any con-flictual situation. Practice seeing both sides with equanimity and a willingness to let things be what they are. This is not a passive stance; it's one of being very choosy about which battles you really need to take on. If a battle appears necessary, try using the "aikido approach" of simply stepping aside and allowing what's coming at you to fall past you. You need not become the object to hit. In this way, you will keep your balance and know "the high road" to take through any conflict that arises.

The following imagery will enable you to transcend any duality. You can repeat it during the month anytime you feel yourself becoming trapped in some extreme one-sidedness.

Finding That "Third and Higher Thing"
A Guided Imagery

Find a comfortable place to be quiet for a while, close your eyes, and take a few gentle breaths. . . . Ponder some situation going on in your life right now that contains an either/or dilemma. . . .

Now, in your mind's eye, image a triangle, with the two opposites of this situation resting at either side of its base. . . . Envision each opposite as a symbol that expresses its character. . . .

Then, watch what happens as they each gradually move up the sides of the triangle toward the top. . . . Note how they behave as they travel to the top. . . .

And see what new symbol emerges spontaneously as the two merge together at the apex of the triangle as "that third and higher thing.". . . This symbol at the summit represents the transcendent point. It expresses symbolically the way to rise to a higher level of consciousness and unify the "either this or that" that existed below. Take some time to interpret the top symbol now. . . .

Reflect upon this one at the top, and see what feelings or insights arise concerning your current situation. . . . When you feel ready, take some time to come back, and write or draw what you received.

Once you've done this, apply this inner message to the current situation and integrate this inner and outer reality.

CHAPTER THIRTEEN

THE EIGHTH SELF PRINCIPLE
"It's not out, but through, that we heal and transform"

Let me not beg for the stilling of pain,
but for the heart to conquer it.

—Rabindranath Tagore

You Can't Talk Yourself Out of Feelings

It's an illusion to think you can just talk yourself out of negative feelings, or that there is some mental instrument or simple affirmation you can feed your brain that will automatically change your emotional responses. These mental tools can change your mind, but emotions function through the law of thermodynamics: they flow, ripple or roar like water and must be accessed and drained out to heal. So, unless you are willing to have a lobotomy, it's better to not depend on your mind to shift your emotions. When we try to talk ourselves out of feelings, they only go into repression and will come out indirectly when we least want them to. Repression is the shadow's playhouse.

Once emotions *are* cleared, the mind works beautifully to undergird our life with new ideas, healthy beliefs, and an attitude adjustment that fits with our new clarity. But rarely does it work the other way around: spiritual bypass is often the result of trying to control one's feelings without ever having gotten all the way through them with compassion and understanding.

Because your emotional body functions like water, whatever emotions build up in our bodies will gently stir us, or erupt like a torrential storm at sea when feelings run high. If blocked, they store themselves in your cells, closing your heart, and giving you the idea that it's not safe or "spiritual" to feel negative feelings such as anger or deep grief.

As stated in the *Newsweek* magazine edition dedicated to "The New Science of Mind and Body" (September 2004), "From anger to optimism, our emotions are physiological states. The brain, as the source of those states, offers a potential gateway to other tissues and organs—the heart and blood vessels, the gut and even the immune system." So we can see how crucial it is to our well-being to heal our emotional body.

A lake with no ripples will perfectly reflect the sky (or truth). Your emotional body, to heal, must use techniques that empty out the feelings with compassion and no judgment. Then, your emotional body will be transparent to meet each present moment with the pristine clarity of the truth of every situation and relationship you encounter, no longer contaminated with old, unprocessed feelings.

There is no such thing as rising up and out of an emotion you've never let yourself feel. Once a feeling has gone into your body, or hit your psyche in any way at all, it won't just go away; it has to be made conscious and expressed in order to release. For emotional healing to prevail, we must find a safe and appropriate place to enter fully into whatever is left unprocessed and ride it all the way through until the pent-up energy is drained off the issue. Then, it is finished, never to command your attention or psychic energy again.

The Nature and Purpose of Resistance

We humans are notorious for resisting pain. When resistance is understood correctly, however, we can learn to respect it as the beginning of change. Something that's been repressed in our subconscious mind is pushing against the walls of conscious awareness now, seeking to be seen and felt through, so it can heal. We might naturally feel fear at first, and try to repress it again. After all, our fear of this feeling is why it was repressed in the first place! So we resist, not knowing what will happen if it rears its ugly head.

Resistance, being the gift that it is, is either coming from your superconscious mind—your higher mind—or from your subconscious mind, your ego's repressed material. If your resistance of the inner work of emotional clearing is coming from your higher mind, it may mean you are not ready to work through this particular issue in your life. Or, the conditions are not safe enough for you to proceed. Then again, the resistance can be a fear of what might happen once you do clear this issue; it might require changes in your life that you're just not ready to make. In such cases, your Self is guarding you from moving too fast, awaiting some favorable changes in your outer world before you go deep into processing unleashed emotions.

Now, if the resistance is coming from a wounded ego stance, holding you away from something you've not wanted to face, or fearing that you may lose control, then the resistance may be coming from a subpersonality who is blocking your growth.

You can find out the origin of your resistance by going inward and imaging a symbol for the resistance. If it's a guide or Christ figure in a white robe, a Being holding a lantern, a rose, a glowing cross, or a serpent encircling a staff—something that represents holy or high—then it's coming from your Self. So you honor the resistance and pray that the feelings will abate. If the image that comes is dark, thick—like a door that won't open or a mud hole, or a sign that says "Danger, don't enter," its energy feels down or heavy, not uplifting or light—then it's your ego telling you to stop your inner work. You may wish to override this resistance and find a safe place to go deeply into the feelings of fear, anger or sorrow that you may be holding, and just let them express so they can "bleed out."

Heavy Hearts Just Want to Empty

The heart grows heavy when it has to hold a lot of unprocessed grief or sorrow or unexpressed anger, fear or frustration. When your heart is heavy it constricts, your breathing becomes shallow, and your life goes flat; you are living on a superficial level, which is never fulfilling. Your life force is being taken up in holding yourself away from your feelings. Your heart just wants to empty. Like wringing out a dishcloth soggy with dirty water, the heart just wants to be squeezed out so it can lighten up and help you feel more alive.

Your heart is not judging what's there; it only wants release. So, without interfering, or commenting on it, or manipulating it in any way, just let the process take hold. In the privacy of your own space, let your feelings rise to the surface. If you feel terribly blocked, music will often help.

Your psyche knows how to release emotional pain if you'll let it do its work. And you'll notice that, as you allow the feelings to flow on out, you are simultaneously observing the stream of events your heart is releasing. Once you recognize that you are the one perceiving this process, you'll realize you *have* feelings, and you are *not* your feelings! Your emotions are simply pointers to unfinished life experiences living in you. As they empty, you'll see that the events that may have hurt you are over; you've already lived through them. All that's left are the memories living in your cells, and in your mind and heart. They are simply pent-up energy stuck in your body-mind.

When you do emotional healing in this manner, you'll discover how to experience naked reality without the mental or emotional veneer you've used to cover it. Once these blocked emotions of pain are released, you will be amazed at how light you feel. You'll feel forgiveness for yourself or others who've harmed you; you'll feel calm and centered. You'll be coming from your heart, the fourth level of consciousness where everything begins to harmonize. And you will feel the bliss of being fully involved in life.

Jesus said, "As a man thinketh in his heart, so is he." When a child, I'd always thought this was a typographical error in the Bible: How can we think with our hearts? At this fourth level of consciousness, mind and heart come together; you think with the nonjudgmental, all-encompassing, receptive intelligence of your compassionate heart.

Released Negative Feelings Turn to Their Opposites

The more completely we can feel something all the way through, the quicker it will release and turn toward its hidden opposite. For example, the more I'm allowed to feel my anger about something, the quicker compassion or forgiveness can pour in. New life enters into an empty space where old, constricted energies are cleared away and a healing has occurred.

Traditional therapies often move in and stop feelings, or even medicate us so we won't feel much at all. Though there are certain instances where medication is useful, it's sad to see so many people walking around with unclear emotional bodies. New-paradigm therapists do not fear feelings and know they are simply crying out to be accessed, owned, felt through and released. We learn to build the proper containers so that we, and those we serve, have a safe place to express our feelings appropriately. It is the "loaded" pent-up emotions that we fear, not natural feelings. When natural feelings have permission to be expressed, there is never any repression; consequently, there is never any emotionalism of extreme needs having to act out. And from what we now know about the shadow, the more we repress our unwanted feelings, the more they will act out in the most inappropriate extremes.

Emotional Pain Is Inherent in This Life

Being human isn't for the fainthearted. Because we live in a dense, concrete reality, this physical life can hurt us badly when a body we love dies or when we hit a wall or catch a bullet or break our neck or lose our eyesight. We live in two worlds at once: this physical reality where all of spiritual existence plays out, and in the archetypal/spiritual reality where we are universally connected to everyone in our species, and to all life.

There is a beautiful Persian poem by Zuleka that states this paradoxical reality so plainly:

"Rabia, Rabia, why are you weeping?"

"I am sorrowing," she says.
"Rabia, Rabia, why are you sorrowing?"
"I am eating the bread of this world,
While doing the work of that world."

This makes me think of Jesus and the Buddha, and other great beings who have come here, knowing full well there is a purpose here that simply must be lived to spiritualize this human existence. When we can access the archetypal significance of some pain we are carrying, it helps mend a broken heart, feeling not alone, in the company of others who have experienced the same hurt.

In my own life, I was once suffering greatly during a musical journey therapy session about the plight of my firstborn diabetic son who has had a trying physical life. I was feeling sorry for myself as the mother of such a sick child. "Why him, why me?" I kept crying out as I clutched my stomach and wailed out my grief. Then suddenly, from within, I was aware my consciousness had left my body and was soaring over planet Earth, seeing all the mothers in the world who had sick children or who had lost a child. It was a blessed moment, hard to describe. I felt a sigh of relief and a hint of enlightenment. I was united with all the mothers of the world. "This, too, is just another human experience! I am not being singled out," I cried. My personal world and the archetypal/symbolic world of meaning had merged for a few moments and brought me this time of healing. And I felt bliss.

I was once told by a teacher that when we can reach the archetypal significance of some personal plight, it unties all the knots on the thread of that particular issue, and the whole thing is resolved, never again to return. It is finished.

Holding Divine Tension Is Emotional Freedom

Becoming conscious *is* suffering, to some degree. With our eyes wide open, and connected to all human beings, we see pain all over our world. We can feel not only our personal pain, but the collective universal pain as well. Suffering is not the goal, though; deepening into life is.

The human psyche brings to us, either through symptom or symbol, as much reality as we can handle at any one time. We take on what we're capable of handling; the rest, we block. Our egos either surrender to this high and holy work or resist and cause us serious emotional strain. All human suffering is the soul's inability to express its true nature—which is divine love, compassion and creative intelligence—in this dense physical world.

Pleasure and pain are one in bliss. Denying neither—this is the activity of the heart. This "divine tension" we are capable of feeling—pleasure/pain, personal/universal—keeps us in touch with our whole nature, our personal joys and sorrows and our love for humanity all at once. The two become a third and higher thing—neither obsessively seeking only the joy, nor wallowing in the sorrow. This is emotional freedom.

THE LIFE LESSON
Dropping Fear of Feelings

As you walk through your days focusing on this Principle of Wholeness, be constantly aware of the feelings that pass through your body. See how much you can handle being fully present each moment to your feeling nature. The lesson here is to realize emotions are a natural part of living. And emotional overreactions are simply reminders of unfinished life experiences seeking completion. If you are to ever think clearly, all stored-up emotions need to be made conscious and set free. You're at a stage on your journey now to learn to never, ever fear your emotional nature or your passions—no matter what kind of intensity you may believe you are holding yourself away from.

When my emotions are stuck in my throat, I know this is a fifth chakra block. My feelings are right on the verge of true Self-expression. So I've learned to let myself make sound—*any* sound that wants to come. I know I need privacy, and I often find this by getting in my car and driving down a country road with music turned to high volume. Then, I just let out the wail or the anger, or sometimes I'm surprised by a sacred chant or strong toning that pours out spontaneously. From your throat chakra, expressing is the key. The feelings are sitting right there on the surface of your conscious awareness. When clear, your throat may just want to sing and shout. Or tears of joy may pour from your eyes.

If the pent-up emotion is in your heart, you are heavy with something and you may not even know the content; you just feel energy clogged up in your chest. If this is the case, then you've let something or someone break your heart. You've either experienced being unloved from someone you care about, or you've been unloving to someone dear to you and are feeling unfinished, guilty or mean-spirited. Either way—since our nature is love—the heart just wants to empty and feel natural again. When clear, your chest cavity will feel light and airy, or a welling up of intense love, gratitude or awe.

Sometimes you'll feel your emotions mostly in your solar plexus, or in the pit of your stomach. If so, your ego has gotten wounded; it has felt embarrassed, left out, or humiliated about something that's happened. Or, it is being reminded of some old childhood wound that has never had a chance to heal. And this same familiar feeling has surfaced for you to now make conscious. In other words, something that's happened is "loaded" with old feelings of abandonment, shame, or of not being good enough. This makes the current insult much more potent than is called for, giving you an overreaction. Your emotional response to this type of insult may have become an emotional addiction. So let your ego talk to you and feel heard. Then find a way to console it. You'll need to practice releasing this old feeling, so its opposite can come to the fore.

Sometimes the feeling will release and there will be no content. This is fine. We don't have to always know what we're upset about. The story lines are not nearly as important as releasing the feeling from your body and your heart. The stories we tell ourselves can, in fact, be addictive as well.

If you are someone who has used sex as a way to feel wanted or attractive, you may have become addicted to a feeling of sexual turn-on when your ego feels wounded. If so, stay very conscious and use your Observer Self to watch out for acting out in ways that violate your Self. These kinds of sexual feelings are not clearly sexual; they are a neediness from never having felt good enough about yourself. Having sex with a loving partner is a beautiful, healing experience. But we all know that irresponsible sexual acting out makes us feel terrible, and often creates a karmic predicament with another soul.

Your Self is calling you to practice remembering that you are *not* your feelings. Feelings churning inside you are simply pointers or reminders that you are "cooking"; something is still unfinished in your process of awakening that requires emotional release. You are carrying a burden that is making you needy and will cause distortions to happen in your relationships until these feelings are emptied. If you are feeling the symptom in any of these three parts of your body—your throat, your heart or your solar plexus—your emotions are letting you know it's now time for you to let go.

Whatever you think you are holding, instead of trying to talk yourself out of it, or thinking you need to hide it, try giving the feeling *full intention* to release. I like to think of setting my clock for 10 minutes and just letting myself go as deeply into the feeling as I possibly can. I tell myself, "Take it all the way through, all the way to the bottom." So it can empty completely. This is because I've learned that the worst feelings in all this world will only strongly release for five or seven minutes at the longest.

Holding yourself away from the feelings is much more dangerous than letting them flow out. As mind/body medicine tells us, not releasing our emotional upsets can even cause physical disease. Safe containers are available in our therapeutic communities to help clear out the debris stored in your emotional body.

The exercise below will help you release any held-in feelings you may be carrying so they can be made conscious and heal. You can use your "little book" to record anything you learn from its expression to gain more Self-understanding.

THE PRACTICE
Focusing on a Feeling

A Guided Imagery

You can record this imagery and play it back or you can have a friend slowly and quietly read it to you, making sure you pause long enough to experience the imagery suggestions.

Find a place to be alone for a while, or with a very close and trusted friend. Put on some gentle, heartfelt melodic music without words, lie down in a comfortable position and close your eyes.

Begin to breathe in and out to the count of seven, balancing your breath, and continue this until you feel the effects of this gentle, balanced breathing. . . .

Now, take your consciousness to the part of your body where

the block is being felt, and enter into it with all your attention, with the full intention of releasing it. . . . Just allow yourself to remain there, focused, until the feeling starts to come forth. . . . Breathe directly into the feeling for a while. . . .

Now, let any words or sounds come that want to be expressed, and don't worry if it makes any sense, just let it come, whatever it is. . . . Stay with the feeling now. . . . Give it full intention. . . . Take it all the way to the very depth of your heart. . . . deepen. . . . deepen. . . . until you reach its bottom. . . . The feeling may change into something else. . . . Just notice whatever comes. . . .

Once you feel it has emptied, take several rapid breaths, like you are breathing in fresh air, and stay with this process for a few moments until you feel completely empty and clear. . . .

Now, turn off the music and, with your eyes closed, stay in the silence for a while. . . . Just let yourself experience how you are now feeling until you are ready to sit up. . . . Take your time. . . .

When you feel ready, come back here and reflect on what just occurred. You may want to write in your "little book" or draw something that expresses what just happened. Or, if someone is present with you, you may wish to process with them, or later with your therapist.

Getting "Hooked" and "Unhooked"
An Ongoing Daily Practice

Anytime you're clearing emotional blocks, it's a good time to really become conscious of what kinds of people or situations cause you to get emotionally hooked, or cause you to detach, close down or withdraw. Some processes really affect you, while others seem to just flow on by.

So in this process of Self-exploration, ask yourself these questions:

- What just got activated that's causing me to feel an emotional reaction? What story or image is in my mind right now?
- Is this a familiar feeling? If so, how long have I had it?
- What is the common denominator that always comes up in situations like this?
- What is it about me that makes this experience even a part of my reality?
- What is its purpose? What am I trying to learn?

Make it a daily practice this month to walk through your days noticing all this. Use your "little book" to write down any processes that contain emotional energy—any "too muchness," either high or low. Emotional attachments of being too high are just as imbalanced as feeling too depressed and empty. Remember, all addictions occur in the extremes.

So let this month be a walking meditation in learning how you experience your emotions, and in finding ways to heal them.

A note about using the Observer Self in emotional healing:

At times you will notice "static" in the communication between you and your Observer Self. Another voice in your head will interfere—one who is highly critical and judgmental—shaming you for some error you've made. This is *not* the Observer Self; it's a subpersonality called the Inner Critic. You're still in your wounded ego. So go higher, and observe this critical voice as well. Who's talking? How long have I heard this critical one fussing at me? Where does it come from? Try to discover why this voice is in your head right now. Is it serving some function? Or is it simply rewounding you? (You'll no doubt find that it's one who's been with you since you were a child.)

Truly Forgiving and Releasing Another

Holding onto anger toward someone who has harmed you takes a lot of psychic energy. You have to shut down positive parts of you to stay focused on these old resentments. It's best to release them—for your own sake.

"But," you say, "this person really did abuse me! She does not deserve to be forgiven. She was a monster who caused us all great harm." This way of thinking contains an error: forgiving people does not release them from their own karma. This is between them and their Creator. Forgiving is a matter of freeing up your own energy, or releasing you to experience greater things. Your forgiving is for you.

Once you start living as your true Self, everyone is seen for who they are and appreciated for their part in this divine world drama we're all participating in—mistakes and all. Sometimes we see that our worst enemies or offenders are our greatest teachers.

Use this month to practice forgiving someone from your past: See them in your mind as who they truly are. . . . Just allow their image to come into your imagination, and see them clearly. . . .

Now, silently, say to them, "I am releasing you from having any effect on my life or my heart from now on." . . . Notice how you feel as you say this. . . . And notice the image or scene that comes forth in your mind as you say this. . . .

Keep repeating this declaration over and over until you feel an actual energetic release.

Finding Your Own Emotional Support

If you are like me, leaping and bounding through constant change, you probably could use a little supportive companionship along the way. Your own Self-understanding provides a cushion—and hopefully this book will as well. The company of others of like mind and intention who are traveling this journey with you, however, is a strong component of your emotional healing. For here, in the fast lane, your world is rarified. Most everyone "out there" is stuck along the way in the ego's world of outer focus, and this journey can get lonely. It's important to stay close to those who are awakening with you.

Once you commit to this way of living, you are in for a thrilling surprise: Your real kin will start to surface all around you. When you meet someone you have a deep soul connection with, you will feel an instant recognition. You will share a quiet knowing that you truly understand each other—a deep, abiding nonattached love. Through these deep connections, your emotional life will become empowered with spirit.

CHAPTER FOURTEEN

THE NINTH SELF PRINCIPLE
"There are no outer experts on a path of Self-knowledge"

I say these powers will be given to you,
but more correctly, you give them to yourself,
for you even now possess them though you
know it not; nothing can be added
from without, all comes from within.

—Will Garver

The Self Is the Only Expert on *You*

On a path of Self-knowledge, there can be no outer experts. Your Self is the only true authority concerning your own nature. Now, isn't that logical when you think about it? All that outer seeking we do eventually leads us right back to where we started—inside our own minds and hearts. There's no place to go; there's simply someone to be. In *The Myth of Meaning*, depth psychologist Aniela Jaffe says, "God creates the Self and then realized Himself through encountering His own creation." So, to say the Self is our teacher is a sacred process, coming straight from our Creator.

The further along we go in our awakening, the more we realize that the journey itself is our home. And as we travel it, the Self teaches in only one way: through the wisdom gained from our direct experiences. Not through textbooks, not through listening to others, but going within and finding the treasures buried in your own psyche—this is how you gain Self-knowledge. All those outer forms of learning can serve to validate what you discover. And it's thrilling to hear about things that you've experienced and know them to be true.

The human/divine Self is designed to reweave the threads that link human thought with soul and spirit—which is what we are doing right now as you read this. Your true Self, as your sacred blueprint, reminds you that you are here to live creatively from center, guided by your own inborn soul wisdom and sense of Self—rather than driven by the dictates and expectations of others. Becoming your own inner "expert" turns you in the right direction to really know yourself. All else is rumor—or someone else's idea of who you ought to be. Even what you are reading in this book needs to be filtered through your own inner "truth detector." If what's being said rings true, by all means, take it in; if not, just let it pass on by.

Following the path of direct experience is a fascinating adventure in consciousness that removes the need for outer experts. Traveling upon your inner landscape thrills your heart and preoccupies your mind so much, you forget to be always seeking answers somewhere "out there." While delving into your true Self's nature, you'll be witnessing and experiencing the deeper meaning of all your feelings, attitudes and beliefs, plus the sacred purpose of your relationships and the events you undergo as you travel along.

The path of Self-knowledge leads to this "world of meaning," where a more in-depth, broader understanding of life is seen. From your inner work, there will be spontaneous openings within your heart or your mind into a level of reality beyond the external—and you'll be bathed in the light of *meaning*. From this inner world that resides closer to our source, we gain a bird's-eye view, rather than the myopic vision we have when we're standing in the middle of our own picture. Meaning is curative in nature, for it gives us a sense of wholeness and purpose. Discovering the meaning and spiritual purpose of our experiences is the awakening; this is the transformation we all seek.

Without a sense of meaning to your life, your ordinary reality unfolds along a crooked, unpredictable line of chance events. You can't see how everything is connected. From the symbolic world of meaning, all your apparently unrelated outer conditions and your accompanying inner feelings group into *meaningful clusters* and make their sacred purpose known. Expanding into the symbolic world of meaning is a movement back to your source, where all patterns of wholeness, including that of your own true Self, are starkly revealed. Through meditation or times of deep contemplation, you can go there anytime you need more understanding of something that's happening to you. In this wider realm of consciousness, your realized Self is both "in the world and not of it." It knows the ways of both this world and the world of Spirit.

Making Your Life a Sacred Ritual

The world around you is alive with synchronistic markers, metaphors, potent symbols and powerful lessons, all of which can teach you something about the fullness of who you are and help you awaken on your sacred journey. Your soul speaks in symbols, remember? Metaphors, parables, images, geometric patterns, numbers, color, sounds, signs and synchronicity are the language of your inner Self.

You can walk through your daily life as a sacred ritual, bowing in gratitude to the symbols you receive, recognizing them as messengers from the soul's dimension. They work like "enzymes" that stir your psyche with deeper meanings than you can know with your intellect alone. You learn to have the eyes to see and the ears to hear as your reality unfolds.

Your incarnated soul directs you in mysterious ways that often puzzle the intellect—through flashes of insight, scenes and images that burst upon your consciousness—all pregnant with meaning. A scrap of paper dancing in the wind becomes a transcendent symbol of beauty that pulls you out of some current despair. The scent in the air triggers a memory that fills in a gap in your current understanding. You read about someone whose life strikingly parallels your own, and you suddenly remember a missing piece of your own story. An owl lands right outside your window and looks in at you right at the precise moment you need to be reminded of your own ability to soar.

"Why did this happen just now?" you ask. "This is a profound metaphor that's showing me the way." Everything that appears in your outer life is a reflection of something in your inner world. Once you understand how this flawless mirroring works, whatever comes upon your path can give your awakening Self a powerful push. You'll see that it's the inner life that is determining your outer conditions, and not the other way around. As you wake up to all the ways your true Self is unveiling, you begin to see the extraordinary in the ordinary everywhere you look.

Because your personality is already linked to the greater Self at the heart of all things, you have the innate ability to view the world from this transcendent perspective. The archetypal Self of Humanity lives in the "world of meaning," a reality closer to our Source than our intellects can normally reach. Therefore, the Self can communicate with this higher way of knowing by reading the symbols, metaphors, and signs and by training your personality to look for the deep spiritual root of every life situation that touches you and everything you do.

Spawning Self-Knowledge

Now, don't panic if you feel you have no experience working with images or interpreting symbols. Studying this book may actually be enough to guide you. I've found that rarely is a professional or a symbol dictionary needed to help understand your inner images when they appear. Dream and symbol dictionaries that provide universal symbol interpretations, or other sources of formal instruction, can even get in the way of a fresh understanding of your own unique inner life and way of knowing. Working with symbols spawns Self-knowledge. The experience of relating to these symbols is itself the teacher. Spend just a few moments with them, enter into them, and become them, and they will teach you themselves what they represent. These symbols are actual psychic entities from your inner life. Just making the commitment to communicate in the "world of meaning"—whether it's through journaling, meditation, group or individual therapy, musical soul journeying, or dream interpretation—will bring you great results.

Once you enter the path of Self-knowledge, it's nearly impossible to any longer lose yourself in others. You become disinterested in dogma, or allowing other people to decide what you are to believe, or what makes you healthy or "spiritual." As you unveil your true Self, you will be less dependent upon others' expertise or validation because you'll gain a whole new sense of self-confidence in your own way of knowing truth. You'll become a free thinker.

Healing Codependence

Codependence has been rampant in our country. It's a flawed model of what was intended to be devotion to God in selfless service. Missing, though, has been the understanding that you have to have a Self before you can give it away! We move from Selfness to selfless, in that order. With no sense of Selfhood, we live someone else's life and spend little time advancing our own. Waking up means discovering your own formula for right living.

Psychospiritual inner work is the healer of codependence. Following the path of Self-knowledge leads to the remembrance that you are part of the Divine, and frees you from the sense of powerlessness in the face of hard trials and difficult decisions. You enter into your own creation story with the confidence of a co-creator. Your focus shifts from outer distractions to painting the beautiful portrait of a Self busy realizing its own potential, and enjoying it immensely. This creative, masterful way of being is your birthright. You are your own most important teacher, and the Self that you cocreate along with your Higher Power is your gift to humanity's unfolding.

THE LIFE LESSON
Committing to the Life You Were Born to Live

The fact that you are reading this book suggests that you have realized that you must follow an inward track to the truth of your being and are willing to learn to trust this inner way. So now is the time to deepen your practice of turning inward and listening to the voice of your own inner Self.

Take stock of yourself to see if there are any people to whom you have given away your power, any "experts" whose views you have adopted without question. Whose life or wisdom do you believe is more valuable than your own? It may be one of your intimate relations, or perhaps a doctor, a minister or a psychic. Be willing to examine any dogma or formula you may have adopted that did not come from within yourself. If you come up with something, ask yourself now whether or not you've reflected on what you've adopted and know it to be *your* truth. And if so, that's fine. Remember that you are capable of "free thought," of fresh thinking.

This life lesson brings you the practice of seeing the world around you as a mirrored reflection of your inner reality. Anytime you need to, you can reach out into the Big Mind of the world and take from it what your individual mind needs to understand. So, take note of this as you walk through your days, moment by moment, making decisions. When you trust the inner life as real, you become a "scientist of the soul." You document your findings by keeping your "little book" and your spiritual journal, recording all that you receive that seems important and noting how the messages provided by the world affect you.

At first you may discount what happens as simple coincidence. But after a little personal research, you'll see that the revelations that come to you through coincidence are "recognitions" that the divine plan for humanity is unfolding through you, as it is through all who are willing to become conscious cocreators.

Perhaps this particular Life Principle is especially relevant for you just now. If so, you are being called to take back your power as a Self-realizing person and know that you are to focus now on developing your own special gifts rather than bowing to others who are already expressing theirs. You may be about to overcome a sense of spiritual inertia by taking a stand and getting busy with the task at hand.

Just acting "as if" you already know that you have a role to play in the world's unfolding drama can jump-start your expression of your own true calling. Notice, too, that you'll start getting feedback from those around you that you've changed, become stronger, lighter, more alive.

The key to this life lesson is learning to live by the wisdom you've gained from your own direct experience of living. You have a "truth detector" inside you. It resides in your heart. Your heart will tell you when you are in the presence of authenticity, and it will go "thud" when you have strayed from your path or fallen into falsehood. Look inside, to the light that shines within, for therein lies the core of the life you were born to live.

THE PRACTICE
Standing in Your Soul's Own Light
A Guided Imagery

Put on some quiet, inspirational music with no words you can understand, and close your eyes and go within for a while. You can ask someone to read this guided imagery to you, or record it and hear it in your own voice....

Imagine yourself standing in a circle of light, facing toward your future.... Let the light penetrate your mind and heart and flood all the cells of your body.... Note how it feels to be encompassed in this light.... Now, realize that this light is coming from your very center, from the realized Self within....

Notice how you feel as you stand there bathed in the light of your own soul.... Notice that you need nothing from outside.... You are complete.... Realize that you always are this light ... and anchor this feeling as the state of consciousness you wish to live as....

Now, come back to this reality and contemplate what just happened in your inner life.... You may want to write or draw for a while to express any insights you gained.

You can carry this image with you now, always, everywhere you go. No one has to know you're doing it. This is a private matter. As you make this process conscious, you'll begin to notice that you can gentle down any negative circumstance you may encounter. When light enters the scene, all darkness or negativity just naturally begins to move toward the center until it vaporizes into what is good, true and beautiful. When you carry the light into any situation or conflict, the darkness begins to dissipate and people around you are affected, though they may not even know it.

As you become a practiced light bearer and take responsibility for carrying it, your light will expand further. Being a light bearer for the world means that you live your truth and tell your truth through your loving heart.

You really are this powerful, if you allow yourself to stand in the light of your own soul ... remembering that nothing can be added from without, all comes from within.

CHAPTER FIFTEEN

THE TENTH SELF PRINCIPLE

"Your Symptoms of dis-ease are not pathological; they are the pangs of birthing a new consciousness"

Our story is a birth. It is the birth of humankind
as one body. What Christ and all great beings
came to Earth to reveal is true.
We are one body, born into this universe.
Go tell others the story of our birth.

—Barbara Marx Hubbard

Your Crisis Is a Birth

In our process of awakening, energies always move in two opposite directions. The higher a tree grows, the deeper its roots. This is how our hybrid nature works. On the one hand we become more of an individual, while simultaneously, we are digging deeply into the collective unconscious mind to gather up our greater Self and our connection to all humanity. A realization of the Self is a feeling of eternity and being beyond life and death. We start to feel more compelled to be of service to humankind, which places us more *in* life rather than being removed from it. Any time our ego overtakes this process, a kind of elitism can creep in when you start becoming conscious, which can become confused with being true to your Self.

The new human you are birthing from your willingness to pursue is a soul-infused personality who thinks about what is good for the whole, while still honoring your individual's needs as well. Through you few are willing to carry this resurrection story to the masses—by birthing your Self—you not only heal yourself, you make universal Divine Love an individual possibility. You learn to live this double life with grace, both as the individual and as a vital part of the collective Self.

With most people, however, there is a problem here: Because most everyone is unconscious of this larger mission and knowledge of our connection with the whole, it has become the norm to take on our conditions, then become identified with them, and take nearly everything that happens to us personally. We completely forget how to release that which we took on to make it conscious. We swim around in the mental constructs, feelings, and behaviors of others, of society, and of our culture, that keep the old patterns in place, forgetting the labors of love that we are each to bring to the family of humankind.

This move toward wholeness is our birthright and a very high state of consciousness. Yet, we often experience this shift to the larger life as a crisis. The ego knows it must sacrifice its selfish needs that do not gratify the soul. Ego deaths are painful, but a necessary element in this sacred human journey. Just always try to remember that when your ego is dying to have something it thinks it can hardly live without, something greater is taking hold. Nothing is ever lost, only transformed into something new. You can have faith that we are always moving toward a greater reality, though often we know it not.

A Vision of the Future

In 1993, I had a vision: I was crawling out of a foxhole, or some type of earth upheaval, and saw myself slowly climbing a hill onto a new Earth, where there was no manmade technology, only nature in the raw. I'd started my climb as a tiny infant, but by the time I got to the top of the hill, I'd become a full-grown woman.

At first, I thought I was alone. And I was sorrowing. Then I looked around and saw that we were *all* there—congratulating ourselves for having completed some very important mission. "We did it!" we shouted jubilantly, as we all ran around hugging one another in celebration. It was as though we all remembered what we'd come to Earth for, and now we'd completed our job, and were heading Home.

Next, I realized the earth from which we'd arisen was bellowing out her gift of song—quite loudly and proudly, in fact. She was belting out a grand and earthy rock and roll. It was gorgeous music—sensual, luscious and vibrant—the beat ever so strong and inviting. Then, I noticed that from the magenta-blue sky in our new world, beings were coming to greet us from the beyond. They were ethereal creatures, perfect and lovely, nearly transparent, with little form. They were barely visible, except for their magnificent eyes. There was a figure in the center who looked to me like the Christ. All were coming toward us.

As the terrestrial and celestial lives began to merge, I noticed those from the sky were bringing their song to greet us. Their music was high and lilting harmonious chords, heavenly and melodic. Though uplifting and gorgeous, their music had little substance, no oomph! It was high and evenly pitched, evoking no human passion.

Then the most amazing thing happened: The earth's lusty orchestral sounds and those of the heavenly choir blended into one symphony—and together it created the most incredible music I've yet to hear with human ears. As the music played, each heavenly guest entered into each of our bodies, and, individually, we amalgamated into one Being. And there we were—a brand-new species. We all turned eastward and started walking calmly toward a new dawn, as though we knew exactly where we were going.

Could This Be Our Collective Destiny?

Perhaps this is not just my story but our human story as well. When our cosmic memory begins to return, we can see that we're all here for a similar reason. The purpose of being born on Earth is to take on the human condition by entering into our particular DNA chain, so we can purify what we can and become the true Self we've come here to be. The family coding we each took on belongs to our specific ancestral chain, which contains specific weaknesses and dysfunction on all three of the basic human levels—physical, emotional and mental "clogs in the machine." Because we accepted this particular family's unredeemed impairments, we're the one who can heal them by making the dysfunction conscious and changing the code.

The only way you can transform an ingrained family pattern is by entering into it, so you can know it fully. When we are gripped by a difficult family dysfunction on any level, we turn toward it and face it squarely in the eye. Now we are taking charge rather than being unconsciously possessed while we were looking the other way. We stop, take note, and look at what is driving us and why. Then, from that place of knowing, we become the change we desire to be. We understand it, heal it, and learn to behave in a whole new way. In this manner, we are each doing "our part" in birthing the new and higher level of consciousness coming into humanity's awareness now.

Labeling Ourselves as Sick or Crazy Is a Curse

It is sad how we pathologize ourselves for having issues in life, or for getting a little crazy sometimes and making embarrassing mistakes. We've come here to do just that! How else are we going to know from the inside out how it feels to be human? We have to get shadowy to understand the shadow; we must experience being inept or ill-prepared in life to know how to be wise. We have to hurt to know what being hurt feels like. How else could we ever develop compassion for another human being if we, ourselves, have not ever suffered or made a fool of ourselves?

Walking around calling yourself sick, with labels that pathologize you, functions like a curse: you will become that which you've been named. This creates an identity crisis for your emerging soul, one that can destroy your motivation to progress toward realizing your full potential. Diagnostics should never be deterministic: they need to flow with us, as we bob up and down through life's trials with the constant pangs of rebirth striking at every aspect of our nature.

You who are the muses of the soul will hear this message with a strong sense of "That's me you're talking about!" "You are verbalizing the meaning and purpose of my life." You passionate ones are the risk takers, willing to step on out to the edge of what we know, and move toward the unfolding of our next state of being. You are the seekers who "go first." Eventually, all humanity will come upon this inner path.

The paradigm shift we're currently making is the shift away from seeing ourselves as bad, wrong or sick. The shift is seeing that we are just naturally struggling to bring in a new way of being, one not tied to the separatist, personal life so egoistically, but to a life more connected to service for the whole. The Twelve Step Big Book of Alcoholics Anonymous says, "Having recovered from a hopeless state of mind and body, we carry this message to those we serve." Having *been there*, we have a message to carry. We *are* the message.

As we each commit to our own healing, we're not only helping ourselves, but all others who have a similar plight. And this is something I hope to pass on to you that you will always remember: Each time any one of you makes something conscious and heals it in yourself, you've created a little more light in the one shared Human Soul in the archetypal, pattern-making dimension of reality. In the ancient wisdom philosophy, this is called "the way of karmic retribution." We take on what we need to in order to heal it, then we pull it out of the human psyche so it will clear out of Humanity's consciousness entirely. We grow into the new Human—or whatever we're to be as our next statement of being.

We Are Never "Just Personal"

Carl Jung once said that we can never separate from our archetypal roots any more than an organ can separate from its physical body. We are that connected to all that is. Therefore, no matter how much we may take things personally, our problems or issues in life are *never* "just personal." This is an illusion, and one many people hold. Remembering to not take things personally is a potent healing factor in our awakening.

Birthing a new consciousness means you are bursting out of an old personality you've outgrown, and are expanding into a wider self. This is emotionally painful, as biological birth is physically painful. Birth is birth on all levels of consciousness—a leaving of a smaller life and entering into a larger one, where the entire foundation of reality is foreign to you. If you can picture yourself having to burst your boundaries, shed your skin, and pour into a larger frame—that's what's happening in your consciousness right now. You are becoming more spacious. You are expanding beyond what has been the familiar.

Experiencing death/rebirth cycles are natural transformational processes that happen to us, whether we like it or not, and whether we know it or not. All ideas of rebirth are founded on this fact. Nature herself demands constant death and rebirth. And *our* nature is included in this demand.

THE LIFE LESSON
Being Too Sensitive or Self-Absorbed

If this lesson speaks to you, then you may be unconscious of the impersonal, collective aspect of some issue that is currently troubling you. Stop and reflect on some serious current issue you're involved in, and see if this is the case. If so, you are taking it personally, thinking only of yourself, and so your emotions are reactive rather than free to act from a clear mind. You are swimming in the unclear waters of a personal melodrama, perhaps even feeling sorry for yourself, or entitled to something better. Notice how hooked you are in this situation—how much you talk about it, feeling like a victim, or making it more of a drama than it truly needs to be. Notice how self-preoccupied you've become. Talk to a couple of friends you trust and ask them how they are seeing you in this particular circumstance. Get an objective view.

I remember once I was furious about an ex-boyfriend whom I was certain had betrayed me. I'd vented on and on with one of my best friends for weeks, by phone, and every time we got together. She'd heard the story over and over, listening patiently with compassion while I ranted and raved and repeated myself *ad nauseum*. Finally, one day she said, "Jacquie, you're about to tell me this story for the fifth time. But if you really need to tell it again, I'll really listen." That was one of the most therapeutic confrontations I'd ever heard. She'd let me know how obsessed I was, and how much she loved me all in one sentence. I did not feel judged for my foolishness. She'd handed me a key.

You took all this on so you could heal it. Remember? Now you've become identified with it. The dis-identification exercise in The Practice for Principle Three will help you here. So refer to it now. Then, here's another practice that will aid you in waking up and stepping out of your current ordeal.

THE PRACTICE
Swimming Through the Sea
of Emotion Without Getting Hooked
A Guided Imagery

As you know, your emotions are "watery" by nature, and when stirred, they churn like a turbulent sea. As long as your emotional body is riled up like this, you cannot see the truth of any situation; you're "hooked" and instead of acting from center, you will *react* from some old pattern, a fragment of yourself still living in the past. You can make a grave mistake if you choose to take action while in this imbalanced state. So you will need to "quell the waters," and come into balance. This imagery will work:

Close your eyes and go into your mind. And with your mind's eye, image yourself in a boat that is tossing around in a turbulent storm at sea. Feel this happening to you, as you strive to balance yourself and save your life. . . . Notice how it feels to be tossed around like this. . . .

Now, make the connection with the problem you are having in your life where you are being so reactive and unclear. . . . Notice who is in the boat with you. . . . And see how you are relating to them and they to you. . . .

Simultaneously, with the problem situation still in your mind, create an image of the waters beginning to calm as the storm ceases and the sun comes out from behind the clouds. . . . Gradually, the waves begin to settle into the quietness of a windless day at sea. . . .

Now, you are floating in the calmness of a pool that is close to the shore. . . . You are anchoring into a safe harbor now. . . . Breathing easy. . . . What had been a terrible situation has changed into one that is completely safe and calm.

As you reflect on the issue at hand, in calmness it's easy now to discern what to do to once and for all resolve this problem situation.

Take some time to feel gratitude for your creative imagination and your Higher Self.

Hanging in the Dangle

An Exercise in Patience

When your old life feels dead and the new has not yet arrived, you learn the art of "hanging in the dangle." This phrase was coined in an interchange with a group of my students in Georgia about 15 years ago. Several in the group had announced that they were living in their cars. These folks had been striving so hard to create new lives that they had made choices that were not logical, giving up their only means of making a living before the new way had announced itself! The frustration in the group was high, when someone who had gone on and on in her complaining finally cried out, "I feel like I'm just dangling in the middle of nowhere!"

"Well, I guess you'll just have to hang in the dangle," I replied with some irritation, which immediately became funny and gave us all a good laugh.

If this feeling of hanging in space between two lives is happening to you right now, get busy learning the skill of how to just hang out in that state of "no-place-to-be." Believe it or not, you can learn to relax into this particular stage on the journey, especially if you have a few loving friends who will support your process and help you feel less anxious or ungrounded.

It helps to envision yourself as the trapeze artist who has let go of one bar and is reaching for the other that is coming her way. Tell yourself that there's a "safety net" underneath you—that if you fall, you'll be caught. This safety net is the context of transformation itself. As you've learned, metamorphosis is movement. You know that no matter what happens, things will change. Even fear or despair will eventually drop away. Later, you'll look back and see that this moment of hanging in the dangle was terrifying but also purposeful and exhilarating. In the "open moment," anything can happen, and something certainly will!

Here is a process that can help support you through this awkward stage:

• Focus with all your might on your spiritual intention.

- Imagine that your personal "vibration" matches the energy of the Higher Power.
- Consciously surrender to this higher vibration knowing that it can move through you.
- Now, just let go.
- Stay "in the presence" of your Higher Power or inner guide no matter what is happening. Trust that the process of new birth is underway.
- Wait patiently and recognize your new life as it begins to "show."
- Be willing to take the first step into your new life, no matter how vulnerable or ill-prepared you feel. Just do it! And you'll be on your way.

Shifting to the Vertical Dimension of Consciousness
An Exercise in Turning Inward

Sacrificing some old attachment or identity can signal a time for turning inward and receiving messages from your soul. Your own consciousness makes a U-turn by shifting from the worldly horizontal plane—that unfolds along a timeline of past, present and future—to the sacred inner vertical dimension that unfolds beyond time and space. When you shift to the vertical perspective, instead of looking outward, your focus is upward or inward.

Here are the steps you can follow if you're ready to make this shift:

1. Find a quiet place where you won't be disturbed, and become very still.
2. Bring to mind an image of your Higher Power.
3. Image yourself standing at the intersection of a cross, at the

point where the horizontal and the vertical lines meet.

4. Look up and offer whatever you are releasing with open hands.

5. Really feel what you are giving up leave your hands.

6. If tears or feelings come, allow them to flow unimpeded until they naturally subside.

7. Thank your Higher Power for this opportunity to relinquish this part of yourself's rule over you, a part of yourself you no longer need.

8. Sit in the void this loss creates and feel the emptiness. Be willing to stay with this feeling for a while.

9. Take a moment to envision yourself living without this attachment.

10. When the time feels right, allow the emptiness to be filled with a sense of joy and relief. Breathe in this lighthearted feeling. Make it real.

11. Now, in your mind, see yourself moving on—lighter, unburdened, free.

A Daily Act of Self-Remembrance

At least once a day, all month, read this paragraph to yourself, and take some time to reflect on who you are, on who you've always been:

"If I can remember who and what I am, and what all of us
are here to be and do, rich memories of an ancient past
and of a still uncarved, emerging future will return
and carry me forward like a shooting star, into the beyond."

"The ancient past" is your cosmic memory, going as far back as the beginning of it all. "The beyond" is that place in consciousness where the creative imagination becomes our only avenue for getting there. It's all the uncarved potential that has never been imagined. Here, we "think it up." And then, we can watch it materialize. As a cocreator, you have that power. This power is always to be filtered through the qualities of love and wisdom.

CHAPTER SIXTEEN

THE ELEVENTH SELF PRINCIPLE

"An open heart is the bridge to the Divine"

Each time we drop our masks and meet
heart to heart, we awaken from our sense
of separateness, which is what
we are called to do in all things.

—Ram Dass

The heart chakra, located in the center of the chest, links our body and spirit and drives the life force that propels our feeling nature. Intuitively, we know how important the heart is, not just to the physical body, but to the soul. When athletes go all out to win, we say that they "put their hearts into the game." When we are devastated by a tragedy, we say that we are "heartsick" or "broken-hearted." When we are moved by a benefactor's generosity and compassion, we describe that person as being "all heart."

Words such as these point to a deep truth that becomes more and more clear to us as our emotions heal and we awaken spiritually. The emotional energy of the heart chakra is a bridge that links us to the higher realms where Divine Love continuously spins creation into being. When our hearts are open, we are filled with creative energy and connected to the pure power of the Source. When our hearts are closed, we cannot access the feelings that come from the spiritual realm. We are devoid of inspiration and the bliss of being one's true Self.

As the bridge between the human personality and the soul, an open heart helps us to heal any split between what is happening in our individual life and what the collective spiritual life is calling us to be or do. An open heart is able to hold "the tension of the opposites" between what is happening to us personally, and its deeper, more universal meaning. We know when we have bridged this gap because we experience a peaceful feeling of warmth and release right in the center of our chest.

For example, say that you're brokenhearted over the impending loss of a loved one who is in the process of dying. You feel your grief as a hollowness or emptiness in your chest. Yet, when you open your heart to a feeling of compassion for your loved one's suffering, your brokenhearted emptiness is held in balance by a feeling of calm warmth toward all who suffer, with a quiet knowing that physical death brings peace to them as well. Similarly, a feeling of intense anger at a friend's betrayal can be held in balance by an openhearted recognition of your gratitude for the lesson you've learned as a result of this experience. In the heart, pain and pleasure become one. We hold on. We release. Fullness and emptiness combine and balance.

The Heart Is Where the Personal and Transpersonal Meet

As our sorrows and our joys mix together, the human personality contracts to the smallness of individual pain and expands to encompass the suffering of all people. Pain and joy are neither wallowed in nor sought after; neither despised nor ignored. Mystics describe this "divine tension" as a state of bliss in which the whole Self is engaged. The personal and the collective combine and rise to the top of the triangle, into that third and higher synthesis, which is emotional wholeness and freedom.

The heart unites while the intellect divides. Heart feeling is the opposite of cool, removed rationality. When we drop the mask of separateness and speak to another person "heart to heart," our common bond overrides any sense of "me" and "mine" and links us as fellow travelers on the human journey. The bridge of the heart allows genuine dialogue to take place and grounds us in the absolute truth of the moment. An atmosphere of unconditional love encourages agreement and gentle change so that everybody wins.

Recently, in a family therapy session, I worked with a father and his teenaged daughter. The daughter had been caught smoking marijuana after school, and the father was so upset with her, he could hardly sit in his chair. The argument escalated as the father shouted his convictions about drugs and the stupidity of kids who use them. The daughter matched his level of distress, shouting back at him about how rigid and moralistic he was not to give her a chance to explain or apologize. The two were so entangled in their rage, I couldn't get a word in edgewise.

Finally, I was able to tell the father to look into his daughter's eyes. As he did this, the energy in the room suddenly shifted. His voice choked with tears, he took his daughter's hand, and said, "I'm not sure I know how to be a good father. I'm just so afraid you're going to be hurt, or that I'm going to lose you!" When she heard this heartfelt confession, the daughter's defiance just melted away. In this communion of the heart, the two fell into stillness and then calmly began working out a plan for resolving their conflict.

Because the heart links our personal experiences of pain, loss, fear, remorse and grief with the higher or spiritual meaning of human tragedy and suffering, it enables us to move beyond any self-centered reactivity. When our hearts are open, we can respond to another's pain with true empathy, experiencing both personal compassion and transpersonal objectivity. Both responses happen at once. Such expansion into the spiritual dimension is the cosmic purpose of personal suffering. We are the only species who suffers, by the way. All species experience pain. Suffering is holding *on* to pain and contains a mental component of catastrophic thinking.

Heartwork Is Holy Work

Heartwork is a universal sacred process known as initiation. The word *initiation* means "to enter into." Simply understood, experiences of initiation move us up the ladder toward becoming more fully realized human beings. We gain wisdom and expand as we travel into knowing more of that which already is. When the challenges of initiation hit, we can choose how we respond. We can close down and contract into a stance of self-absorbed grief or angry projection and blame. Or, we can struggle to hold the tension between our personal feelings and the larger meaning of what is happening to us. What is the lesson here? What is my soul wanting to teach me? Or, perhaps, what is my soul wanting to experience?

We have a mission to fulfill. Our task is to prepare ourselves so that the Divine can flow through our personal human experience and out into the larger world. The process of initiation allows us to enter into a state of grace in which we are available to the deeper meaning of whatever we encounter. Human Initiates are seasoned souls who never fear the cycles of death and rebirth. They are always open to new feelings, new ideas and new paths. Surrendering to the Divine within and allowing Spirit to guide their lives is their natural way of being.

The key to experiencing life as initiation is holding the heart open. A closed heart walls you off from access to the higher dimensions in which the creative imagination, inspiration and intuition can be accessed. Shaken by the fear of change and death, you peer with vacant eyes at a threatening world full of uncried tears, repressed anger and unexpressed caring. Spirit is unable to flow through repressed feelings that close the heart.

The open heart, on the other hand, allows life experiences to work their transformative magic of healing and awakening us. With an open heart, we think as our Creator thinks and feel as our Creator feels. An open heart is expansive and free. When your heart is unclogged and standing free, you just naturally stride fearlessly through whatever life presents. Spirit blows through you, and you see in your mind images of your new life, new possibilities beyond your current limitations. Seeing life through the eyes of the soul, you become an agent of inspired ideas and free thought. No longer burdened by heavy judgment and the world's opinions, you can remain transparent, so that the winds of Spirit can blow through you unencumbered.

THE LIFE LESSON
Coming from the Heart

When you live "from the heart," you can relax and just be yourself. You have no ax to grind, no position to defend, nothing to hide, no one to impress. Coming from the heart melts your negativity and collapses all one-sided judgments, fanatical beliefs, and any need to be acknowledged as good, or right.

A heart that is contracted is full of anger or resentment toward someone and it will eat up your precious energy. These feelings turn to depression at some point and can make you sick. It is critical to your well-being that you learn to release anger and resentment—not to let someone who's harmed you off the hook—but for your own sake. When you give a person who has caused you pain back to God, you liberate your own psyche and have more energy available for your own advancement along the path.

A wounded heart closes up to protect itself. Sadly, too many of us have become experts at feeling wounded. We hug our experiences of abuse, addiction, betrayal or childhood trauma close to our hearts, as if our wounds are our primary identity. Our woundedness becomes an addiction. Many people live in this closed state their entire lives. When the heart clogs up for long periods of time, something big often has to happen to "blow it all out" and once more open us to life. Serious illness, especially heart attacks, may be one form this "blow out" takes. Paradoxically, it's often in crisis that families come together in love, and much healing and forgiveness happens when the wounds of the heart are openly shared.

If this Principle is speaking to you, you may be living in denial about the effects of some unhealed heart wound you're carrying in your body. You may be blaming someone in your current life for a past hurt that you've been unable to heal and integrate. Getting clear about what's past and what's present is the first step in healing this problem.

Take a moment and ask yourself what emotional hurts you may still need to heal. Whom do you still need to forgive? Can you love yourself enough to work through any unfinished business from your past and move on into the present? No one can clear the "fog" off your psyche's mirror but you. Sacred heartwork may require that you call a friend or family member and set up a time to engage in a heart-to-heart dialogue about any unfinished processes still living between you.

An unhealed wound from the past may also cause you to "protect" yourself so as not to be wounded again in the future. Ask yourself whether, and in what ways, this may be true for you. Are you holding yourself back from some new opportunity that is inviting you to step beyond your familiar ways because you are scared you won't measure up? Or do you fear being hurt? Did some authority figure in the past make you feel as if you'd failed? Or, are you scared you may have to give something up you feel you cannot do without?

Remind yourself that it's natural to feel anxiety when you start to expand beyond your usual parameters. Opening your heart to compassion for yourself can help you stand in the tension of not knowing how things will turn out. Think of how courageous you've already been to have made it to this stage of awakening. Know that it's time now to trust the process of evolution to carry you forward to your next right place. I've learned that when we do our part and be open, God will do the rest.

As you practice the work of coming from the heart, one day you will see that you've developed the ability to live from the heart in all situations. You will have stepped out from behind the veil of superficiality, no longer afraid to truly be yourself. You know people who behave this way. So do I. They are a joy to be around and model for us the beauty of authentic living.

The following practices can help you clear the wounds of the heart and move you toward this more open and courageous approach to life.

THE PRACTICE
Breathing into the Heart

Find a place to sit comfortably for a while, and close your eyes, focusing on your breath. Gently breathe in and out to the count of seven (at your own pace).... Feel your breath begin to balance.... And notice how your body begins to let go and relax.... Now, check and see if you have any constriction or tightness surrounding your heart.... And quietly breathe your in-breath into your heart space, feeling the warmth of the breath start to dissipate any tightness or tension collected there.... Feel this warmth begin to spread out throughout the trunk of your body, until you feel spacious and open.... as though you are empty and transparent.... Allow this feeling to spread now all over your body ... until you feel perfectly relaxed and open.

Now, imagine this heart warmth beginning to spread beyond your body into the space around you.... It's spreading now to all those whom you love....

Feel it now begin to spread throughout our world, to everyone or anyone who needs the touch of a loving heart.... Stay with this feeling until all is perfectly calm.

Come back to this reality, and take some time to integrate this process. Know you can repeat this exercise anytime you feel your heart constricting.

Surrender into Love

A Guided Imagery

Read this exercise all the way through before you practice it. If music helps to activate your emotions, put on some evocative music without words, close your eyes, and allow yourself to go quietly into your feelings. . . .

Feel the sadness or hurt, the fear, the sense of betrayal. Whatever is in your heart, let it come. . . . Now, give yourself permission to grieve your feelings in any way that feels appropriate. Cry, beat a pillow, shout at the heavens, make low groaning sounds coming from deep in your chest. . . . Since anger may also be involved in your feelings, express your anger in some harmless way. . . . Yell, stamp your feet, or dance out your fury. . . . Allow all of the energy of any feelings you may have repressed to move through you and out now. . . .

As you bring the emotion through, imagine that a soft white light is entering your heart from "the sky of mind." See that your mind is connecting with your heart, inviting it to relax and open. Concentrate on this light flooding into your heart until you experience a gradual lightening of your feelings. Using your creative imagination, continue to let your heart fill with this light until you are completely relaxed and calm.

Now, stay with this feeling of lightness and release until your chest cavity empties and you feel transparent. . . . Take as long as you need for this process to subside. . . .

Let the music play for a while now, and when all your emotions are clear, notice how much lighter you feel. As you go back to your usual routines, you may notice a dramatic improvement in your emotional responsiveness and your clarity of mind.

Any time you feel that your heart is clogging up with unexpressed feeling, know that you can repeat this exercise in emotional release.

CHAPTER SEVENTEEN

THE TWELFTH SELF PRINCIPLE
"As you cultivate your own nature, all around you begins to grow"

As I went by a pitch-pine wood the other day,
I saw a few little ones springing up in a pasture
from seeds which had been blown from the
wood. . . . In a few years, if not disturbed, these
seedlings will alter the face of Nature here.

—Henry David Thoreau

Your Hard-Earned Growth Is Contagious

By your willingness to know your Self, you have emerged as one
of these seedlings who will alter the face of nature here. In *The
Gospel According to Thomas,* Jesus reminds his disciples:
"Whosoever knows the All but fails to know himself lacks every-

173

thing." This statement has now come home to you as a truth that you will share with others.

The growth you have achieved is contagious! The seeds of wisdom, beauty and love that you have planted as you have walked the path of direct experience have been gestating underground, in the dark "night world" of your consciousness. Watered by experience, nurtured by heartfelt Self-awareness, these seeds of your own future flowering are now ready to burst into bloom, with your heartfelt energy spreading to everyone you come in contact with. As your emotions have cleared, you have cleansed the fog from your inner mirror and brought your energies into balance so that you can begin living as your true Self. No more excuses! You are simply you.

When your life is guided from within by the high Principles of the Self, the extraordinary shines through the ordinary everywhere you are. This brings a sense of sacred meaning and purpose to all of your activities and helps to materialize Spirit in this human world.

The secret of true service is simply this: Develop your own soul's qualities to their highest level, and the light of Spirit will express itself through everything you do. In this way, everyone who comes upon your path is served just by being in your presence. People will just naturally feel good about themselves when surrounded by your energy field.

Every great soul who has inhabited this planet did their ultimate service by simply being fully and completely themselves. What each of us learns from our own direct experience, we have to give others, so we become guides along the way. We don't guide because we are superior to others; we guide because we are familiar with the inner landscape and we are not afraid of what we meet there.

Whether you realize it or not, by just being yourself, you will be modeling for others how to be less identified with the personality and more centered in the awareness of the soul. If you've done your homework, your intuition will now be flooded with ways to transmute the energy constricted in a negative habit into its positive quality that was hidden underneath its misuse. You'll know how to "change lead into gold."

The Seven Stages of Creation

Everything you wish to create from now on will come into being through a series of seven steps, beginning at the highest chakra and proceeding downward. Remember, all new creations emanate from Source:

- First, through the seventh chakra, you conceive the idea received from the Self.
- Second, at the third eye, your sixth chakra, you envision whether the idea will be good for all humanity. If you see that it's not, you will abandon the creation, realizing it didn't come from Spirit.
- Third, you use your creative imagination to transform the new creation into a formulated thought, putting language to it and naming it, from the throat, or fifth chakra.
- Fourth, you surround your new creation with an impassioned love and the protection of your heart, as you would a precious child, desiring with all of your might that it grows to healthy fruition. This is the function of your fourth chakra.
- Fifth, at the solar plexus, your third chakra, you begin to devise concrete ways for this creation to manifest.
- Sixth, at the power center below your navel, your second

chakra, you attract the helpers and tools that you need for bringing the new creation into form.

• And finally, at the first chakra, you birth or build your creation in the world, with a deep sense of gratitude for the help you received "from above."

As a newly awakened cocreator, you can practice these steps until they become second nature, so that birthing a new creation happens through you like magic.

Your Service Is Simply "Doing Your Being"

Often, we labor under the mistaken notion that true service requires that we always put ourselves last. And though that sounds very unselfish and high-minded, to live in selfless service before you've become a Self is a violation of cosmic law. Until you have a strong sense of Self, you have no Self to give away. It's your responsibility to meet the needs of both your personality and your soul. This culminates in service naturally, since your service is "being your Self." Once you've become a Self, the "selfless" stage happens naturally with no thought, as there is no ego noticing it.

The path of Self-knowledge can never be learned from just reading a book. By your own conscious participation in life, as you've seen in these pages, you learn to adapt to, integrate and transcend your evolving identities as you take them on, and then, like skins that have become too tight, shed them so that you can expand. As you trek along, you will constantly be leaving the lesser for the greater Self. There will always be some part of you that is now too constricting to contain your expanding Self. The Self must use your personality's nature as the raw material for transformation. Otherwise there's nothing for it to work with, no dross to turn into gold, no "grist for the mill." And so goes the process of becoming whole.

Sadly, many people get so captivated by their involvement in the mundane activities of the material world that they completely forget to focus on the real reason they're on this earth. Then as their life nears its end, they cry in bitter despair, "Is that all there is? Where did the time go?"

To learn to live as this paradoxical one who is both human and divine is your highest realization as a spiritual being in human form. This realization brings a strong sense of Self-empowerment and just enough humility to keep the ego in check. I hope this book has brought this truth home to you. As you learn to honor both your inner and outer life as sacred and to travel *consciously* on your life journey, you start to thrive on the adventures in consciousness that come your way. This way of living is true freedom. For, no matter what life brings, you see its sacred purpose, appreciate it, and learn what you can from it. Judging things as good or bad tends to fall away. Life just is. Things just are what they are.

We all can manifest a life of personal joy and fulfillment if we're willing to keep growing and cultivating the qualities of the soul. The secret that completes any human journey is this: When you are willing to focus intently on cultivating your own nature, everything else falls magically into place. Even when you don't realize this is what is happening, as you remain true to your course, you walk through your life in unique expression as a "demonstrator of the Divine."

THE LIFE LESSON
Donning the Mantle of Self-Empowerment

The key to this lesson is letting go of any preconceived notions about who you are and what you can be. You're being called to see your life in the light of the timeless Now. You know that you have the power to heal the wounds of the past by clearing your emotional body and redefining whatever has happened to you as a necessary step in your evolution. When you travel inwardly, you harvest the wisdom of experience gathered during every day of your earthly life. You can decide that each painful experience was a lesson designed to make you more skillful, more compassionate or more authentic. Reframing your past in this way honors all that you have been and clears the way for your rapid progress toward your desired future for us all.

Accepting the mantle of Self-empowerment means you have no more excuses about not being the one you came here to be. All subpersonalities have come under your Self's compassionate control, and through this Principle, you are called to stand tall in Self-remembrance. You are living from your bigger story now, knowing you are participating in a divine play of consciousness in which you have an essential role. When you accept the mantle of Self-empowerment, your human biography will merge into the wider story of humanity's unfolding, and you will feel an intrinsic part of the human community. No longer will you take things so personally. And this will free your emotional body from any lingering self-doubt.

You are called now to go about your business right at that intersection between your ordinary human affairs, and the ever-present Now of the Divine. Each day, you move up and down along this vertical axis of consciousness—sometimes dipping down to pull something up from your unconscious mind so that it can be acknowledged and healed; sometimes soaring into the cloudless sky of spiritual vision and ecstasy. Going down to pick up some lost part of yourself is as sacred as soaring in the heights. All inner work furthers your integration and expansion.

THE PRACTICE
Becoming a Demonstrator of the Divine
A Guided Imagery

As small children, we still retained our cosmic connection with Spirit. But as we grow and enter fully into everyday tasks, our cosmic memory starts to fade. When ordinary reality seems to be all there is, and those soul events during which everything shines with Spirit seem few and far between, you may need something to help you remember your greater identity and your real story. Whenever you feel the need to remind yourself of who you are in your fullness, you can use this simple exercise to banish any doubt or sense of limitation:

Close your eyes and imagine that you are sitting outside on a beautiful starry night. . . . Feel the night breeze on your cheek and relax into a state of peaceful contentment. . . . Take as long as you need to imagine yourself fully into this scene. . . .

Now focus on one particular star in the indigo blue sky and imagine that it is so bright you can reach out and touch it. . . . See this star becoming brighter and brighter and beginning to move toward you. . . . As it comes closer, enfolding you in beams of love, see that the star is really your own divine Self, the fully realized one that all of your hard work on this sacred journey has brought to fruition. . . .

Now this Star-Self is merging with you and infusing you with light. . . . And you see the world you inhabit through new eyes. . . .

Joined with the light of the Star-Self that you are, you easily see your life's work and sacred purpose. . . . You see your part in the Divine Plan unfolding before you . . . and understand the role you are to play in helping humanity blossom at this particular time in human history. . . . Imagine that now, with all your might. . . . Your vision even allows you to see humanity in full bloom. . . .

Now, just let this image take you wherever it might for a little while. . . . Put on the mantle of your true mission and purpose for incarnating here on earth. . . . Take as long as you need to anchor this knowing in your mind and heart. . . .

When you feel yourself coming back to ordinary reality, take a few moments to note in your journal what you have seen.

Then, in your mind, stand at the "nil point" and banish all self-doubt from your consciousness! Doubt is the final barrier you must cross before you can come home to your Self. You no longer need to carry old mental attachments. No blocks or negative thinking can stand in the way of your fulfillment as a human soul. Never forget that whatever is happening to you, you are a demonstrator of the Divine! The full blossoming of humanity depends on you, along with all your fellow travelers here on planet Earth.

CHAPTER EIGHTEEN

THE JOURNEY IS OUR HOME

People are used to thinking that anything higher
than they has to be divine beings—that is,
without a body—who appear in a burst of light.
In other words, the gods as they are conceived.
But it isn't like that at all—a new mind is being
formed. And the body is learning its lessons—
all bodies, all bodies.

—The Mother

In this final chapter, I'd like to remind you of our bigger story, to put everything concerning our little individual lives into perspective, and to prepare you to proceed in grace along your way.

You've become familiar now with the Principles of the Self that govern your journey. As you move forward beyond the study of this book, it will be your delight to live up to them. You'll discover they function as "seed thoughts" that take root and grow into your own ideas anytime you need them. When you apply these Principles to your daily life, you'll find that you start to accelerate in spiritual stature and psychological health. They honor your human/divine hybrid nature in truth and will keep you "on the mark."

Many people today believe we are to reject our humanness to be spiritual—to just rise above this worldly life entirely and dissolve into light. There are spiritual paths that teach us to work hard to leave our bodies so we can be "just spiritual." This is a dangerous misunderstanding that takes us in exactly the opposite direction for Spirit to manifest in concrete form. We already are the light. We're here now to *embody* Spirit, to bring our God-nature fully into human form and into this physical existence. Trying to rise up and out of our human nature, as though it is bad or wrong, is a blasphemy of our Creator God. It violates humanity's sacred purpose for coming to Earth. It says we are God's mistake!

Instead of concentrating on leaving life, we are called to live life to its fullest while here in human bodies. And as we travel along and learn the bad, the good, the right, the wrong; all dualities become that "third and higher thing," the oneness that incorporates and heals all the splits within us. Then, through this deep psychospiritual inner work, transcendence happens naturally, with nothing left unintegrated.

As consciousness, we are the evolutionary process itself. And since we are infinite, eternal beings, the journey is neverending, so there is no place to "arrive." The journey itself is our home. It's where we live and move and have our being. Currently, there is a dual transformation occurring here on planet Earth. Both the body and the consciousness of humanity are moving up a notch on the evolutionary ladder. This means that the human cellular structure as well as our minds and hearts are literally changing form. And we ourselves are the new creation.

Your sacred purpose is the same as it is for everyone who lives in a human body: We are all to fully engage in our humanness, and bring Spirit's ways to every part of this human life. Once we complete the human experience, we'll be beginners all over again, participating fully in what comes next. Following this amazing mystery of creation is the most exhilarating adventure in consciousness we could ever imagine. Who could dream up a greater "high"?

Through this, our own creation story, we are growing into a new Self, one who is capable of adapting to the new conditions here. And the new keynote for humanity, if our species-type is to survive, is "unity in diversity." It enables us to keep our individual uniqueness, while remembering that we are one. Ponder these three words, and you'll see that living by this all-inclusive maxim will not only heal us, it will heal our world, and end all wars.

By becoming your new Self, you are aiding in the one Soul of Humanity's sacred initiation. This is "the Great Opus" of human unfoldment of which the alchemists of old spoke. Living your ordinary life with this sense of high purpose expands your consciousness and enables you to more readily release any dysfunctional behaviors that are blocking your growth. As a planetary worker in service to your Creator, why would you ever want to live as less than you are? As you travel your journey, you are not just building new skills at living; you are transforming yourself into a whole new being.

Never get caught up, though, in attempting to arrive. For, no matter where you find yourself at any given time, there is no place to go, there is only someone to be.

Materializing Spirit Is Your True Calling

Our Creator *spiritualizes matter.* As God's offspring, we are here to *materialize Spirit.* We are God's cocreators who incarnated, not to leave the human kingdom still half-made, but to complete it. Being fully human is therefore the most sacred act we can ever do. And what a mystery that is. We still have no idea what we'll be once the human kingdom is perfected in nature. Perhaps this is when we'll bring heaven to earth. What a blessing to be participating in such a cosmic event!

To regress a moment: There are four kingdoms in nature. The mineral, plant and animal kingdoms came before us and have already completed themselves. The human species is the fourth kingdom that arrived in nature when the human psyche was born—when we were given minds and hearts that can emote, think, plan, dream and cocreate. Just look at God's handiwork of diamonds, crystals, amino acids, fruits, vegetables, blossoming flowers, medicinal herbs, and the perfect beauty of the various animal species. Who has not been aware that cats are truly gods? (Just ask one!)

We've assimilated the three kingdoms below us; they allow us to thrive in our animal bodies. Now, we are moving evolution forward by manifesting Spirit in human form. But we humans are still in the making. Having had the Way modeled for us by beings as great as the Christ and the Buddha, we all still have a way to go. Once our emotional bodies purify and our minds become clear, we will just naturally be that unique, ideal Self we each came here to be. And when we all do this, our species will reach fruition.

Never forget that as God's child, you carry the seed of creation within you. And this seed, you now know, is the Self—your unique portrayal of the archetypal Self, the human blueprint. We were never intended to be helpless creatures relying on God to take care of us. Living as conscious cocreators is our job description, and no one can do your part but you. As you make the Self legitimate—*by just believing in it and allowing it to express through you*—you'll start to see that anything about you that is not of Spirit's making will start to dissolve. You will simply lose interest. This is how consciousness works, because once you make something conscious, it's very difficult to go unconscious around it anymore. Becoming conscious absolutely ruins your ability to enjoy abusing alcohol, drugs, people or processes here.

As cocreators, once we become conscious we'll see that our egos require discipline, while the soul only needs to express. To set the ego aright, and heal it of any wounds it has accumulated while developing, we require a daily practice that keeps us on the mark. Like pieces in a jigsaw puzzle, we all have our part to do in making up the whole picture of a spiritual humanity. When we don't fill in our piece, or we try to lean on someone else's piece, the puzzle has a hole or a lump in it that ruins the entire picture.

Your Own Personal Evolution

So now, apply this greater cosmic process to your own personal life. You will see that you, too, are still in the process of coming whole. Accepting yourself as just where you are on your journey is another vital component in healing your psyche. It removes shame and blame about the mistakes made or the problems encountered along our way.

To materialize Spirit—think about it—what would you look like? It would mean that everything you engage in is imbued with Spirit's essence. This is where your soul comes in. When we bring the essence of our soul into all our activities, we are fulfilling our purpose here. Remember, your soul is the bridge between Spirit and matter, and *it is formless qualities only.* Your soul's nature is light, which is the whole truth of anything seen clearly. It is innocence, beauty, goodness, joy, compassion, all your heartfelt feelings, love, spontaneity, childlike wonder, intensified sensuality, inspiration and delight. Just watch a three-year-old child. When allowed to just be natural, a small child shows us how the uncontaminated soul behaves in a human body. "Except ye come to me as a little child, you cannot enter the kingdom of heaven." "And a little child shall lead them."

Your Descending/Ascending Self

To materialize Spirit, we move into experiences here, take them on fully in the outer life, and live it to the hilt with our eyes wide open: We consciously descend into matter. Then, we pull out and ascend by turning inward to assess and integrate what we learned. What was loving and led to good? What was harmful and didn't work? We assess, correct, refine and practice what we learned. Through this process of self-reflection, we develop the quality of spiritual discrimination and take responsibility for the choices we make.

The question that's so difficult will always be, how much do I take on before I release my attachment to it? "Too muchness" is holding on to worldly things beyond their usefulness. Once known all the way through, the experience turns negative if we remain attached. This is what addiction is—too much of something. Yet, "too little" doesn't work, either. Then, we leave behind something not yet made known and integrated. And I guarantee you, it will return again and again *ad nauseum* until we learn the lesson. Your Self demands completion.

Staying tuned in to your sacred purpose as many hours of the day as possible enables you to release what's over with, and enter into the new with the confidence of your true Self. As the Self, you'll be able to use good timing about when to leave and when to stay, and transform whatever you've taken on into something positive and purposeful. You can always know when something's finished—be it a habit, a relationship, a career choice, a geographic location—because it will feel dead. That feeling of deadness indicates that the soul got bored and left. You gained and gave all that was possible in that experience. So your job will be to step out of it with love and gratitude for what the experience brought you. Then you are free to move on to the next attraction. Stay in touch with your soul's bliss, and you'll stay on your path.

Healing the Emotional Body Purifies Your Passions

Your passions and strong interests become your bliss when brought forth in truth—especially for you who are muses of the soul. But it must be your *real* passions, and not artificial or temporal substitutes or distractions the ego gets attracted to. These unhealthy compulsions or addictions are merely the human trials we undergo as we "clean up our act" and travel our road toward our complete unfolding.

We all have wounds and distortions in our ego nature. So hopefully we can forgive ourselves and one another in true compassion as we move toward our full healing. It's pretty obvious that we can no longer live as mere egos battling each other to get any selfish needs met. Doing so not only destroys you and me, it will eventually destroy this world.

All pain and suffering here are the soul's inability to express. That hole in the middle of your stomach is really a *whole crying out to express;* it's your soul urging you to express your true desires. As cocreators, we have free will. So it's up to us to bring compassion and forgiveness into all our activities and relations. Shame and blame will dissolve into Self-acceptance and gratitude for all you've learned and for all those who've helped you. You'll see that sometimes your worst adversaries were your best teachers. So all is forgiven, even the abuse. And what freedom this brings!

Unforgiveness is a detriment to our spiritual well-being and to our physical health as well. It produces a potent mixture of stressors such as bitterness, hatred, hostility, anger, resentment and fear of being hurt again. Research has shown that both belligerence and quiet desperation put our hearts at risk. We now know that depression and heart failure are linked. People who are heartbroken die at twice the rate for heart-attack survivors.[13]

Living as our whole nature, we come to understand that the purpose of our human experience is to allow the soul to shine through our physical being in all our affairs, so that heavenly joy and earthly pleasure can be felt as one.

The Inner and the Outer Are One Life

As we consciously advance along the path of direct experience, we learn to honor the inner and the outer, the light and the dark, the divine and human aspects of our nature as one.

Only a spiritual psychology that takes into consideration our hybrid nature as being both human and divine can help us evoke the positive and the possible within us. Otherwise, we're trapped in ego-dominance and a limited definition. Together, the outer-directed ego and the inner-directed soul make up the Self in its full and glorious expression. Never forget that you are all of this.

You can always know how your inner spiritual life is going by examining your outer life. How are your relationships doing? Are you expressing your true life's work? Have you gotten covered up with nonessentials? Do others treat you with respect and gratitude for your being in their life? Are you self-sufficient or still dependent on others to make you feel okay? Do you bring love and acceptance to all your involvements? Are your emotions balanced, or do you still have too many outbursts, fanatical thoughts, or too much self-doubt, neediness, or depression?

Living as Your Greater Self
Becomes Your Spiritual Practice

Having gotten caught up in humanity's unredeemed conditions has been the messy part of our job. We are all in the process of stepping out of our conditions and remembering who we truly are. Enough is enough. It's now time to let go of the hold our past conditioning has on us and practice living in the present moment as our true Self. Your true Self is just awaiting your recognition of who you came here to be. When you are no longer identified as "that one with all the problems," your issues will magically start to disappear. Life on earth will always have sorrow and pain. Yet, the lens we wear as we experience this life makes the difference in how we live through these natural human afflictions. Living as your true Self is your ultimate recovery.

Your willingness to allow your Observer Self to keep you conscious will carry you far, and in an accelerated fashion. Living in two worlds at once—as both the Experiencer and the Watcher—is your hybrid spirit-matter nature in operation. Watching life from the stands while simultaneously being on the playing field leads not to passivity, but to new ways of being. To remember that you are the true Self and not the one who is wounded is your birthright, and why you came into a physical body in the first place. Your job is to "eat the bread of this world while doing the work of that world," as an old Sufi poem reminds us. Keeping these two states of being in balance is your task.

Get up every morning, go outside, face the rising sun and say: "I am willing to do the work of Spirit today." Then, let your day unfold with your Observer Self sitting quietly on your shoulder, noticing what you do as you do it. Keep your "little book" close by so you can jot down any emotional upsets you experience during the day, processing them for only your eyes to see. Go to bed each night having reviewed your day, to make sure you completed anything that still feels unfinished. And call for your inner Guide to bring you a big dream, so you can travel upon your wider terrain where you soul lives and serves Spirit in the night worlds.

If you do nothing else but this, you'll find yourself becoming the conscious cocreator you've always been, but perhaps hadn't fully realized. The Self, our human soul, is rapidly coming into embodiment now, desiring only one thing: to manifest itself concretely through us as the completed Human.

And so ends this tale of your sacred journey through our human unfolding. Or is this simply the turning of Destiny's wheel, a new beginning in your neverending adventure as consciousness itself?

APPENDIX
ONE

Resource Information and Examples
of Transformational Methods of
Healing and Spiritual Renewal

Some of these psychospiritual processes you can do by yourself. Others are offered in workshops and spiritual retreats throughout North America:

- reading books of living truth that speak directly to the soul
- chanting
- drumming circles
- breathwork
- yoga: hatha (physical), bhakti (emotional), or raja (mental)
- contemplation to poetry reading
- movement and sacred dance
- ceremony and ritual
- sweat lodges
- walking the labyrinth
- acupuncture treatments
- various forms of massage and body work

- in-depth Jungian analysis
- symbolic artwork
- dream work
- centering prayer
- exploratory hypnosis
- creating sacred space for spontaneous mystical states to occur
- rites of passage

As you trek along in your healing journey, you'll start listening more to the voice of your soul. It will guide you to where you need to be at any time along your journey. But learning to trust listening to your own soul, rather than being told what to do by others, is a process in itself that requires practice and validation. You'll need to become familiar with how your soul speaks.

For Resource Information

Feel free to contact us at Eupsychia Institute for suggestions on where to find psychospiritual methods of inner work. They are too numerous to list here. Contact us at: Eupsychia Institute, P.O. Box 151960, Austin, TX 78715; (800) 546-2795; (512) 327-2795; e-mail: *eupsychia@austin.rr.com*; or visit our Web site at *www.eupsychia.com.*

Jacquelyn is always willing to respond to you by e-mail. Write her at *jacquie@austin.rr.com*. She loves to hear from her readers.

ENDNOTES

1. Gareth Knight, *A Practical Guide to Qabalistic Symbolism,* vol. 2 (York Beach, Maine: Samuel Weiser, Inc., 1965), 8–10.
2. Candace B. Pert, Ph.D., *Molecules of Emotion: The Science Behind Mind-Body Medicine* (New York: Scribner, 1997).
3. See Paul H. Ray and Sherry Ruth Anderson, *The Cultural Creatives* (New York: Three Rivers Press, 2000) and Richard Florida, *The Rise of the Creative Class* (New York: Basic Books, 2002).
4. See the works of modern physicists Fred Alan Wolf and Fritjof Capra; consciousness researchers Charles Tart, Candace Pert, and Michael Talbot; and integrative medical pioneers Larry Dossey, Christiane Northrup, and Andrew Weil, to name a few.
5. See the writings of Roberto Assagioli in the area of Psychosynthesis.
6. In the author's book, *Transformers: The Therapists of the Future,* the seven levels of consciousness are compared in depth with the Hindu chakra system of meridians throughout the human body.
7. Robert Lee Hotz, "Music Changes Links in the Brain," *Los*

Angeles Times, Dec. 13, 2002 (research quoted from University of Wisconsin, University of Ohio, and Dartmouth College, as published in *Science*). See also Joseph J. Moreno, "Ethnomusic Therapy: An Interdisciplinary Approach to Music and Healing," *The Arts in Psychotherapy* 22, no. 5 (1995). See also Johnathan Goldman's *Healing Sounds, a Spectrum Interview* by Rick Martin at *www.healingsounds.com.*

8. Candace B. Pert, Ph.D., "Molecules and Choice," *Shift* (The Institute of Noetic Sciences Magazine), no. 4, September-November 2004, 20-24.

9. T. T. Gorski, "Relapse Prevention in the Managed Care Environment," GORSKI-CENAPS. 2001 http://www.tgorski.com/gorski_articles/relapse_prevention_in_managed_care_environment_010610.htm. National Institute on Alcohol Abuse and Alcoholism (1989). "Relapse and Craving," *Alcohol Alert,* 6, http://www.niaaa.nih.gov/publications/aa06.htm (Accessed July 7, 2004.) J. M. Polich, D. J. Armor, and H. B. Braiker, "Stability and Change in Drinking Patterns," in *The Course of Alcoholism: Four Years After Treatment* (New York: John Wiley & Sons, 1981), 159-200.

10. See Candace B. Pert, *Molecules of Emotion.*

11. Scientists and academicians in the movie "What the ?!*#? Do We Know" (Samual Goldwin, 2004) explain in detail how our emotions are biochemically shaped and modified by our beliefs about reality. When an emotion heals, the neuropeptides and receptor cells are put back in order.

12. Herbert Benson, Mind/Body Medical Institute, Boston, MA. Research findings quoted in *Newsweek* magazine, September 2004.